D0204085

The Making of a Myth:

THE UNITED STATES AND CHINA

1897–1912

THE
MAKING OF A MYTH:
THE UNITED STATES
AND CHINA

1897–1912

BY PAUL A. VARG

GREENWOOD PRESS, PUBLISHERS
WESTPORT, CONNECTICUT

Library of Congress Cataloging in Publication Data

Varg, Paul A
  The making of a myth.

  Reprint of the ed. published by Michigan State
University Press, East Lansing, Mich.
  Includes index.
  1. United States--Foreign relations--China. 2. China
--Foreign relations--United States. 3. China--Foreign
relations--To 1912. 4. United States--Foreign relations
--1865-1921. I. Title.
[E183.8.C5V3 1980]   327.51073   79-25619
ISBN 0-313-22125-1 lib. bdg.

327.51
V297

Reprinted with the permission of Michigan State University
Press.

Reprinted in 1980 by Greenwood Press, Inc.
51 Riverside Avenue, Westport, CT 06880

Printed in the United States of America

10 9 8 7 6 5 4 3 2 1

To Helen, Again

ACKNOWLEDGMENTS

THE AUTHOR is indebted for cooperative assistance to the staffs of the Michigan State University Library, particularly Henry Koch and Eleanor Boyles, the National Archives, and the Library of Congress. He owes a special debt of gratitude to Professor Sergey Andretz who translated great numbers of Russian documents, and to Dr. Lyle Blair, who over the past several years alternately needled and encouraged the author to continue his research and writing when the pressure of other duties seemed to forbid scholarly research. He is likewise indebted to colleagues who kindly read portions of the manuscript and offered helpful criticism. The author also wishes to thank the *American Historical Review* for permission to reprint a revised version of the article "The Myth of the China Market" which appears as Chapter III in this volume.

CONTENTS

The Making of a Myth:

THE UNITED STATES AND CHINA

1897–1912

CHAPTER I
A STIRRING OF INTEREST

Except for the last two decades, the attitude of the American public toward China combined elements of paternalism and a benign sentimentality. This attitude took shape, in considerable part, in the period 1897 to 1912. It persisted in various forms down through the years and repeatedly confused public debates on what American policy should be.

The complexities of the China question began to appear in the 1890's when China first faced internal pressures toward modernization and when the aggressiveness of western nations threatened to destroy her. By 1912, when the Manchu Dynasty came to an end, a set of public attitudes toward her and an official U.S. policy had taken shape. The two were not identical and this fact provides the theme of this analysis.

The somewhat mystical feeling of friendship, on the part of the Americans, was nourished by sympathy for the Chinese who were suffering the pains of transition from a decentralized agrarian society to a modern state. The periodic floods and droughts that led to heartbreaking famines likewise evoked compassion and these happenings received much publicity, thanks to the drives by the churches for money to provide relief. The imperialism of European states and then of Japan led to a view of the Chinese as people who had given no cause for harsh treatment and yet were subjected to humiliation and abuse. They were the victims of aggression.

The other side of this picture was one of Americans taking pride in their own restraint and philanthropic works. Friends of China, especially missionaries, could say that the United States had seized no territory and had sought to restrain the nations who did. On so many occasions had Americans condemned the aggression of others that they came to believe they had stood in the way of aggression. American philanthropic work, largely through the churches, had built hospitals and schools from simple village ones to more than a dozen colleges. Individual Americans had labored heroically to introduce improved methods of agriculture. However limited in scope or deficient in quality these enterprises may have been, each of them had its supporters in the United States and taken together they symbolized what many Americans so much wanted to believe—that relations between nations could be at a higher level than self-interest and could, in fact, be guided by the principles laid forth in the Sermon on the Mount. The United States, isolated so long from the tense rivalry of nations and richly endowed in natural resources, making possible rapid economic growth, had little experience of the struggle for power. Consequently, it was relatively easy to put ideals above self-interest.

This orientation flourished in an atmosphere where almost no questions were asked. Much of what was written about missionary philanthropy was written by participants and often for the purpose of promoting the cause at home. Consequently, Americans were led to believe that the philanthropy accomplished much more than it actually did. The missionaries themselves hardly seemed fit subjects for criticism and if the schools and hospitals were pitifully inadequate, few knew of the deficiencies. Not until the late 1920's was there any loss of faith in the work and not until the extensive *Laymens' Inquiry* of 1932 was there a hard and objective assessment of the strengths and weaknesses of the missionary enterprise.

Nor was there any sophisticated understanding of how little the philanthropic efforts were geared to meet the aspirations of the Chinese. They sought political control over their own country and this meant freeing themselves from the unequal treaties. They wished to become the masters of China's economy and this meant at least full sovereign power to control foreign enterprises. They longed for the day when no foreigner could treat China as less than equal. Because only a few individual Americans ever grasped the dimensions of these aspirations, it was possible for the average American to believe that the vast multitudes of China recognized that the United States was their friend. Henry L.

Stimson, Secretary of State in the Hoover Administration, explained that in refusing to recognize Japan's conquests in Manchuria he was moved by a knowledge of the

> incalculable harm which would be done immediately to American prestige in China and ultimately to the material interests of America and her people in that region, if after having for many years assisted by public and private effort in the education and development of China towards the ideals of modern Christian civilization, and having taken the lead in the movement which secured the covenant of all the great powers, including ourselves, 'to respect her sovereignty, her independence and her territorial and administrative integrity,' we should now cynically abandon her to her fate when this same covenant was violated.[1]

Genuine goodwill on the part of many and a most natural desire to lay claim to virtue obfuscated the realities of the relationship at the level of people to people. This level of relations received more attention than their official counterpart between Peking and Washington and therefore helped to foster the illusion that the same spirit of philanthropy characterized diplomacy. Students of diplomacy did not confuse the two types of relations, but many of them were, nevertheless, influenced by the nonpolitical orientation. Their very criticisms of the China policy of Washington indicates something other than a realistic approach to diplomacy. Criticisms centered on alleged failures to support China against European Powers and against Japan. Only a very few scholars questioned the importance of China in terms of the national interests of the United States. Almost no one betrayed anything less than a friendly feeling toward China although very few demonstrated respect for her.

Yet, generally, Americans, except at times of crisis, remained indifferent and uninformed. They did not take China seriously, as is indicated by the paucity of attention given to China even in the periodicals whose audience was the better educated upper income group. However, the absence of hostility except on the immigration issue permitted the devoted believers in China to go on believing.

It is when one seeks to understand official relations and the attitudes of the policy-makers that one discovers a dichotomy between the views of the American public and government policy.

To a considerable degree, scholars in writing about American-Chinese relations have blended the public's benevolent feelings with the official policy. This confusion is understandable. The key terms of U.S. policy toward China implied a concern for China rather than a concern for American interests. Diplomatic notes and policy statements reverberated with the benevolence suggested by such phrases as "the Open Door" and "China's independence and territorial and administrative integrity." These conveyed to those uninitiated in the language of diplomacy that the United States had accepted China as a ward to be protected from the evils of European and Japanese imperialism.

Given this hypothesis it was the concern over economic opportunities in China and security considerations that served as the motivation shaping U.S. policy. The importance of these varied from time to time and from one administration to another but neither factor was preeminent over any long period. Neither the economic nor the security factors were of sufficient immediate importance to impress upon statesmen a sense of urgency or of the necessity of taking uncompromising positions. Those charged with the conduct of relations chose to retreat when involvement in the China question verged toward a showdown.

However, even if the stakes had loomed more immediately important in terms of the national interests of the United States there were other barriers to risk-taking. One of these was the American tradition of unilateralism as opposed to entangling alliances. In some specific situations that could have taken shape—danger to American citizens or an attack on the Philippines—unilateral action supported by a public outburst of injury and humiliation could probably have carried the day. These did not occur and consequently the barrier against dangerous involvement held.

Other obstacles had a sobering effect. Policy-makers faced the fact that the Government in Peking was not a reliable partner in diplomacy. It suited the convenience of foreign statesmen to speak of China's sovereignty, her administrative and territorial integrity, her independence, and to address Peking as if that Government presided over China in the same way as the Governments in western capitals preside over their territories. The fact was, however, that China was not a nation-state and her Central Government found itself incapable of dealing with the provinces as subordinate units. Consequently she could not deal with Foreign Governments as if she were an equal and as a result her only weapon was to play one nation against another. Diplomacy is always a two-way affair and those who carried on diplomatic relations had to take into account the nature of China.

Traditional China was not a nation; it was the remains of a civilization. "Peking," said the Chinese, "is far away"; meaning that the authority of the Central Government only on rare occasions significantly affected their lives. The Middle Kingdom constituted a civilization whose unity lay in a common value system based on Confucianism, the overpowering dominance of the family over the individual and the regulation of economic activities by craft and merchant guilds. It was a highly decentralized society based on agriculture, the means of livelihood for more than ninety-three percent of the people. The villages (ten thousand of them) were the major political units.

Confucian ethics dominated society. The rules of conduct and the system of man's obligations constituted a monolithic value system. The moral obligations outlined by the great sage assumed the essential goodness of man and attributed right behavior to enlightenment in the realm of the ethical principles laid forth in the ancient classics. By means of the civil service examination system, knowledge of these classics was widely diffused and successful mastery of Confucian tenets was virtually the only road to preferment. Chinese society rested upon these moral teachings rather than upon law or the use of force, and the ideal of justice illuminated man's intellectual quests. Confidence in achieving the good society by means of the right political structure was notable by its absence. The prime article of faith held that society was only as good as the individuals who composed it.

Given this social philosophy, the Government in Peking could perform only limited roles. The Emperor ruled by the mandate of Heaven. He served as the link between the people and the great unknown, performing a series of religious rituals and exemplifying the virtues outlined by the sages. Numerous boards and the censorate aided him in governing, and he presided over a vast bureaucracy. He appointed the Governors and Viceroys who presided over the provinces. He was at one and the same time an arbitrary ruler empowered to issue edicts having far-reaching effects and a ruler whose powers were carefully circumscribed by traditions more binding than constitutional barriers to arbitrary power.

The splendor of the Court in Peking contrasted sharply with its severely circumscribed powers.[2] Power resided elsewhere. China was above all a decentralized government, and it was in the humble village with its council of elders that the peculiar genius of Chinese political affairs manifested itself. Ideally, the village councilor did not acquire his right to sit by election but by long-demonstrated character, good judgment and virtue. He, like the bureaucrats above him, represented an aristocracy of merit. When the local magistrate, appointed by the Central Government, looked at the village council, he did so recognizing that the council enjoyed an authority firmly embedded in the esteem of the people. So that neither side in the negotiations would run the danger of challenging the authority of the other, the negotiations were carried on through an intermediary. The village elders thereby avoided denying requests from on high as their wishes emerged in modifications of varying degree but always in harmony with their own interests. Thus, as a Chinese scholar phrased it: "We somehow managed to 'hang up' the centralized power so that it did not reach the ground, ..."[3]

The system of collecting taxes similarly bowed to local interests rather than risking a direct challenge of deeply rooted authority. Local officials collected the revenue, adjusting their demands to local conditions and then passing on to the higher authorities the minimum required. The limits on the amount of revenue that could be expected were established more by custom than by arbitrary assessment of needs at the capital, although pressure on the peasants was consistent. This pressure increased sharply after 1900 when the Dynasty launched its program of modernization.

Judicial procedures and the system of law harmonized with the traditional decentralization of power and reaffirmed the basic tenets of a society that aimed at coupling social position and individual merit. The family was the major means of social control. Both law and the courts were reserved for the lower classes—of course, they constituted the great majority—and the low estate of police and judges and the employment of brutal forms of torture in determining guilt reflected the casual contempt of those whose status placed them above the law and yet held them to greater obligations. When a family failed to discipline its own members, it suffered disgrace. The ultimate penalty of the delinquent was expulsion from the family, thereby reducing him to an outcast barred from social amenities and from desirable employment. The official class was above the law and escaped the brutal arbitrariness. The system functioned so effectively that neither police nor courts were important.

The Taiping Rebellion in the middle of the nineteenth century led to further decentralization. The provinces mustered against the rebels the defense that Peking failed to provide, and at the close of the conflict many provinces had their own armies. An equally important transfer of power was the establishment of *likin,* an internal tax, collected by the provinces during the rebellion.[4] Having once gained fiscal autonomy, the provinces maintained it. Finally, provinces began to establish their own mints, setting a precedent that an increasing number of them adopted during the closing decades of the century.

The rebellion's impetus to regionalism coincided with the culmination of a shift in the nature of scholarship beginning during the Ming Dynasty. Scholarship previous to the Ming was broadly ethical in its teachings and relevant to the problems of the day. It became increasingly devoted to minute problems of textual criticism and questions of philology. Scholars' interests had no relevance for society. Rather than fulfilling their former provocative roles as the interpreters of values and as the critical thinkers who distilled the best of traditional thought and applied it in new settings, the scholars divorced themselves from realities. They found their satisfaction in mastery of obscure problems of an academic nature and took pleasure in their escape from the mundane.[5] Thereby, Chinese society lost one of its dynamic elements and the machinery of governing became increasingly bureaucratic, unimaginative, and incapable of creative confrontation with dynamic western nations.

This simplistic explanation does violence to the complexities of Chinese history and her social order. It makes no mention of the long history of peasant revolts or the infinite number of riots, many of them supported by secret societies. Neither does it make reference to the hardships of the masses. The French historian, Etienne Balazs, put it this way:

> The bureaucracy was a hard taskmaster, and its tentacles reached everywhere. It marked every member of society and every sphere of life with its stamp. Nothing escaped it; for the least deviation from prescribed paths had to be kept in check lest it should lead to rebellion, and any dislocation, however slight, was a threat to the system as a whole.[6]

This political and economic order rendered China largely ineffectual in dealings with the nation-states. Each of them dealt with Peking in a haughty spirit. Only the rivalry among themselves and the treaty system served as curbs on their actions.

Beginning with the Treaty of Nanking at the close of the Opium War, the Powers, including the United States, negotiated a series of treaties with Peking regulating relations between China and the outside world. Under the most-favored-nation clause the privileges accorded to any one nation became the privilege of all. These treaties provided for extraterritoriality so that foreigners were not subject to the laws of China and when they were charged with an offense they stood trial before the Consular Representative of their own Government. The tariff on imports was likewise set by the treaties. Foreign residence, except in the case of missionaries, was limited by the treaties to those cities China had agreed to designate as open. Even within these treaty ports foreigners could only reside in the districts set aside for them, a limitation that gave rise to the concessions within those cities where the foreigners were in full control. Shanghai presented a special case. By the 1842 Treaty of Nanking, Shanghai was declared open to foreigners. Great Britain then leased an area bordering on the old city. This leased area became the famous International Settlement which was governed almost wholly by foreigners, a kind of state within China.

A second part of the treaty structure related to missionary work. In response to a request from the first French envoy, an edict was issued in 1844 calling for toleration of Christianity. In 1858, largely as a result of the work of the American missionary,

Samuel Wells Williams, by that time serving as interpreter for his country's diplomatic mission, the religious toleration clause was incorporated in the Russian and American treaties with China. The clause did more than protect Christian missionaries, it extended protection to Chinese converts. This remarkable intrusion of Foreign Governments into the relationship between the Chinese and their own Government opened the door to endless difficulties. Williams wrote: "It must be said, moreover, that if the Chinese had at all comprehended what was involved in these four toleration articles, they would never have signed one of them." [7]

The third facet of China, affecting her relations with western states, was a deep-rooted and pervasive hostility to foreigners. Legations in Peking devoted much of their time to seeking protection for their nationals. Not all foreigners met with hostility; indeed, a majority testified to friendly receptions throughout a lifetime of itinerant preaching in the remote areas while some related incidents when Chinese friends interceded to rescue them even though to do so endangered their own lives.

These facts do not contradict the assertion that the hostility toward the foreigner was so deep and widespread that in all probability his presence would not have been tolerated except for the superiority of western military force.

Alexander Michie, an Englishman living in Tientsin, discussed the subject in a pamphlet entitled "Missionaries in China by a Candid Friend." Missionaries, he said, liked to attribute hostility to the upper classes. Michie labeled this a convenient fiction. He considered it "a daring discrimination for foreigners and strangers to make in any country, that of drawing a line of demarcation between the feelings of the articulate and of the inarticulate sections of the people." He believed that "considering the essentially democratic basis of Chinese polity, and how the educated class is recruited from the *bourgeoisie* and even from the peasantry, no one would come to the conclusion *a priori* that the learned would be likely to nourish feelings which were essentially unpopular."

Michie acknowledged that foreigners moving about the country were seldom molested and might even find sociable traveling companions. "Yet the universal tendency for mobs to gather round stray foreigners," he pointed out, "the rough way they press upon travelers even into the rooms of their inn, the volleys of foul epithets and even of clods and stones always ready to descend on the slightest suggestion, seem to betray a sub-stratum of ill-feeling covered by a very thin crust of civility." "Children of three years in country villages lisping opprobrius names the first time they see a foreigner," he wrote, "tell a tale which can hardly be misunderstood as to the real chronic feelings of the populace." Missionaries, he observed, made genuine friends among the converts but then "those natives who conciliate the missionaries lose caste among their own neighbors."

He identified the hostility as race hatred, a trait found around the world; "and of all peoples on the face of the Earth the English-speaking races have the least reason to be surprised at finding it among the Chinese." [8]

What Michie said is underlined time and again in diplomatic correspondence and in no single decade more amply illustrated than in the 1890's. Charles Denby, the U.S. Minister to China, devoted much, perhaps a major portion, of his time to seeking protection for missionaries. In a lengthy presentation of February 11, 1897, Denby called on the Manchu-Chinese Government "to hold her officials including Viceroys and Governors responsible for outrages on foreigners" and demanded punishment for guilty or negligent officials. When the Chinese turned aside his plea, he accused them of inconsiderate treatment and of disposing of the demand curtly and cavalierly.[9] He wholly ignored the Chinese view that to have demanded of the local officials harsh measures would have reduced them to contempt or worse still, have discredited the already weak authority of Peking. "What I desire China to do is to make anti-foreign riots impossible," he told the Tsung-li Yamen.[10] He warned that now that China was a member of the family of nations, she could not afford to undermine her reputation abroad. He urged:

A ringing earnest proclamation sent to every Yamen in China that not only degradation from office, but condign punishment will be awarded to every official high and low in whose jurisdiction an anti-foreign riot shall occur, would be hailed by the world with joy, would ensure peace, and would save you in future annoyance and loss.[11]

Denby's sucessor, Edwin Conger, was likewise constantly engaged in seeking protection for Americans. However, he rejected Denby's approach and informed the Secretary of State of the futility of making such demands on the Chinese Government.[12]

The policy of the United States toward China in the mid 1890's can only be understood if one keeps in the forefront the decentralized political order, the treaty system, and the anti-foreignism. These three conditions explain the unique pattern of relationships that had developed. The aim was clearly to open China to western trade and cultural influences and to do so regardless of Chinese feelings. The relationship was not that of two sovereign states dealing with each other as equals but rather of a powerful unified nation dealing with a government that presided feebly over a congeries of parts. The treaty system was itself a recognition of the inequality but it was the only way in which there could have been any relations. Consequently the treaties were upheld and served as the guide not to be questioned. The hostility of the Chinese and their contempt for the strange and, from their point of view, inferior western culture confronted by an equally self-confident western civilization, provided the backdrop for diplomacy whether American or European.

In the period 1897 to 1912 new forces portended an end to this relationship. The beginnings of a new relationship began to emerge, yet old habits of thought prevailed on both sides. Although many Chinese now hoped to incorporate the science, technology and military instruments of the West, Peking remained pitifully unable to govern effectively, and therefore neither the United States nor any other nation could look to the Central Government with any confidence that it could protect their interests or promote the economic development that would enhance opportunities for trade and investment. The Foreign Powers with important interests therefore pursued other methods in seeking to achieve their goals. The United States, prevented by her own traditions from entering alliances and inhibited by the absence of any widespread conviction that Chinese interests were worth a strong posture, fell back on setting forth principles to which she hoped others would rally and to giving moral support to those nations who appeared to hold aims similar to her own. How little a sentimental public knew of all this.

NOTES

1. Henry L. Stimson and McGeorge Bundy, *On Active Service in Peace and War* (New York: Harper and Brothers, 1947), p. 90.
2. In a summary description of China's traditional government, brevity is achieved at the price of danger of overstatement and certainly at the cost of oversimplification. This is particularly true when describing the political traditions and institutions. Hosea B. Morse put it this way: "The government of China is an autocratic rule superposed on a democracy; but 'the East is East and the West is West,' and, having applied Occidental terminology to an oriental system, it becomes necessary to define the terms." Hosea Ballou Morse, *The Trade and Administration of China* (Shanghai: Kelly and Walsh, Limited, 1913), p. 32.
3. Hsiao-Tung Fei, *China's Gentry: Essays in Rural-Urban Relations* revised and edited by Margaret Park Redfield with Six Life-Histories of Chinese Gentry Families collected by Hung-teh Chow and an introduction by Robert Redfield (Chicago: University of Chicago Press, 1952), p. 82.
4. Franz Michael, "Military Organization and Power Structure of China during the Taiping Rebellion," *Pacific Historical Review*, XVIII (November, 1949), 469–483.
5. Ping-Ti Ho, *The Ladder of Success in Imperial China: Aspects of Social Mobility, 1368–1911* (New York: Columbia University Press, 1962), p. 11 and Liang Ch'i-ch'ao, *Intellectual Trends in the Ch'ing Period* (Cambridge: Harvard University Press, 1959), *see* introduction by Benjamin Schwartz, p xix.
6. Etienne Balazs, *Chinese Civilization and Bureaucracy: Variations on a Theme*, trans. H. M. Wright (New Haven: Yale University Press, 1964), p. 155.
7. Frederick Wells Williams, *The Life and Letters of Samuel Wells Williams, LLD* (New York: G. P. Putnam's Sons, 1899), p. 271.
8. Charles Denby to Secretary of State James G. Blaine, April 5, 1892, Department of State Archives. Denby transmitted the pamphlet.
9. Denby to Tsungli Yamen, July 10, 1897, Department of State Archives.
10. *Ibid.*
11. *Ibid.*
12. Conger noted: "You will observe from the correspondence that the

Tsungli Yamen flatly refused to comply with Minister Denby's suggestions in this regard, and when he reiterated them, his note was never answered. Nothing short of an exhibition, and I believe the actual employment of force will ever constrain the Imperial Government to punish such officials. It seems to me, therefore, unwise to insistently make demands, which we know will not be complied with." E. H. Conger to Hay, February 13, 1900, Department of State Archives.

CHAPTER II
THE BEGINNINGS OF A NEW RELATIONSHIP

ACCORDING to the general appearance of things in the early 1890's, China would gradually modernize, trade would grow, and the Imperial Government would acquire those attributes of sovereignty required to take its place in the modern world. The peaceful and orderly transition envisaged reflected the current faith in progress rather than the realities of the painful historical process. The traditional Middle Kingdom was, instead, on the edge of a cataclysm, the reverberations of which would be felt for generations.

It is one of the ironies of history that just as the Empire entered upon the convulsive throes of death and rebirth, segments of the American community bursting with confidence, came to the conclusion that the United States could hasten the process and shape it to its own ends. This confidence flowed from the amazing success of Americans in building the greatest industrial machine in the world and in expanding cities and states across a continent that had been primeval wilderness only a few generations before.

Without this self-confidence, Americans could not have entered the scene of turmoil in Asia so lightheartedly and so unaware of the possible consequences. The more immediate causes of their decision in favor of involvement ranged from a mundane interest in China as a future market, to a dedication to the building of a Chinese society infused with Christian values and humaneness, and to concern that a modernized China would align herself with Russia and endanger western civilization.

The commercial argument outweighed the others if the measure is the frequency with which it was repeated in public speeches, Congressional debate, and in certain periodicals. The argument gained strength by virtue of a widely held concern that the major economic problem facing the United States was over-production. David Wells had emphasized the crisis brought on by technological advance as early as the mid 1880's in his widely read book, *Recent Economic Changes and Their Effects on the Production and Distribution of Wealth and the Well-Being of Society.* The depression years of 1893 to 1897 increased the fear of surfeited home markets and increased the interest in foreign markets. It was likewise popular to argue that the best prospects for markets abroad were those areas not yet preempted by the advanced industrial nations of Europe. Representative William Sulzer of New York sounded a popular refrain when he told Congress during the debate over the annexation of Hawaii:

> Let me say to the businessmen of America, look to the land of the setting sun, look to the Pacific! There are teeming millions there who will ere long want to be fed and clothed the same as we are. There is the great market that the continental powers are to-day struggling for. . . . In my judgment, during the next hundred years, the great volume of trade and commerce, so far as this country is concerned, will not be eastward, but will be westward; will not be across the Atlantic, but will be across the broad Pacific.[1]

The analysis did not accord with the findings of J. A. Hobson whose *Imperialism: A Study* was soon to be published in England. Nor did it accord with the diagnosis of economic ills set forth by many agricultural and labor leaders although some of the spokesmen of both groups gave the theory credence. However, it was so widely accepted that it must be looked upon as one source of motivation for a more energetic conduct of foreign relations.

Part of its acceptance was due to the gains made in sales of goods to China during the 1890's and up to the close of the Russo-Japanese War. Exports of illuminating oil increased from 10,732,819 gallons in 1888 to 40,377,296 gallons in 1894.[2] By 1900, exports of cotton cloth to China reached a figure of 182,023,681 yards and a value of $8,785,134.[3] In 1906, exports of uncolored cotton cloth totaled $29,377,179, or more than eighty percent of the total export of these goods.[4] All in all, the United States exported some $43,660,764 of domestic merchandise to

China during that year.[5] These statistics buoyed up the hopes
for the future; the fact that they were misleading escaped notice.

The happenings on the missionary front in the 1890's were
no less impressive. American Protestant missionary endeavors
were meager before 1890. In that year, there were only five hundred and thirteen American missionaries in China; by 1900
there were more than a thousand.[6] The movement for foreign
missions turned into a crusade with the organization of Student
Volunteers for Foreign Missions in the summer of 1887 at North-
field, Massachusetts. Dynamic personalities like John R. Mott,
Robert E. Spear, Sherwood Eddy, Henry Luce Sr., and Horace
Pitkin inspired a generation of college students with a new and
all-embracing vision of the world. In recalling his days at the
Union Theological Seminary with Pitkin and Luce, Eddy wrote:
"When I would box every afternoon with Pitkin and when we
would run our daily mile in the gym or the open air, we would
say, 'This will carry us another mile in China.' " Eddy noted:
"China was the goal, the lodestar, the great magnet that drew us
all in those days." [7]

This picture of China soon gained wide acceptance. It was a
picture of intriguing contrasts, of an able and industrious people
and of a social order that held men in ignorance, superstition,
and poverty. Liberate the energies and the talents of the three
hundred and eighty million Chinese by the infusion of new
ideals, education, science and technology and they would make
use of their country's great natural resources and become one of
the most powerful of nations. A major theme of the missionaries'
reports was the admirable qualities of the Chinese people.

Arthur H. Smith, long time missionary and a prolific writer
on Chinese life, thought one of the most admirable traits of the
Chinese was an ability to face repeated tragedies with good
humor.[8] The cruelty of natural disasters and personal tragedies
were accepted as tricks of fate and accepted with good grace.
Although missionaries liked to attribute most social ills to what
they described in too simple terms as ancestor worship and crude
superstition, they also stressed the personal qualities of the Chinese. The Reverend John L. Nevius, a missionary in Shantung
and a most sympathetic and thoughtful observer, found the Chi-

nese to be honest and having high moral standards.[9] Gilbert Reid, a missionary whose special assignment was to work with the literati, thought no nation stood as high in its ethical system and he testified that he had never found in the cities of China "such vileness and debauchery as you can find in the slums of any of our large cities in the United States of America." [10] The Reverend F. F. Ellinwood praised the aggressiveness of the Chinese and he maintained that China was the most frugal and industrious of all nations.[11] Bishop William Bashford, who went to China in 1905 after serving as President of Ohio Wesleyan University, praised their virility and industry, intelligence and reasonableness, adaptability and cheerfulness, solidity, common sense, and religion.[12] Like Arthur H. Smith and scores of others he admired their readiness and cheerfulness in adapting themselves to their environment.

This praise of China and the Chinese leavened the dreariness of the situation portrayed by other American observers. Certain missionaries, trained in Bible-centered seminaries, wrote Fletcher Brockman, recalling his own early education, approached China expecting to find the people there, as in all non-Christian lands, in the manner of St. Paul's description:

> full of envy, murder, debate, deceit, malignity; whisperers.
>
> Backbiters, haters of God, despiteful, proud, boasters, inventors of evil things, disobedient to parents,
>
> Without understanding, covenant-breakers, without natural affection, implacable, unmerciful:

This was the picture, said Brockman, that had been given to those who volunteered to become missionaries, and they quite naturally found that China confirmed this.[13] They consequently emphasized the evils they found and some of these appeared so to them only because of their own parochialism.

This missionary picture of China led Americans to approach that country in the spirit of the reformer, committed to its importance but unprepared to accept it as it was. Those interested in China were prepared to enlist the American Foreign Service as an ally in bringing about the kind of China they envisaged and thereby China, to a degree unrivaled by any other country, enjoyed the advantage of a lobby that was manned by Americans who did the work of God and at the same time worked for China.

And there were the intellectual leaders, men of far ranging conjectures about the world that was emerging, men like Brooks Adams and Admiral Mahan. Their thoughts, too, turned to China, and their proclivity for speculation in the grand manner led them to deal with the changing configuration of world power. Upon the nature of the emerging China would depend the security of Anglo-Saxon civilization.

In his provocative analysis of the emerging world power structure, Brooks Adams argued that the benign international order of the nineteenth century rested upon the economic power of Great Britain. This economic power was now in the process of disintegration due to changing patterns of world trade and the decline in importance of West Indies sugar on the world markets. The production of beet sugar in Germany and the coming of the Industrial Revolution to the German states signified the shift of the economic center of the world in an easterly direction. Adams saw Russia emerging as an industrial nation and with this the center would move still further eastward. Control of China by Russia would seal the dominance of the East. To this dreaded specter, Brooks Adams saw only one alternative, the movement of the United States, in partnership with Great Britain, into China and other remote areas. Therefore, the United States must plunge into the rivalry of the European Powers in Asia. It would be developments in China that would determine whether a higher or lower form of civilization was to dominate the earth.[14]

Alfred Thayer Mahan, naval historian and strategist, devoted himself quite as assiduously as did Brooks Adams to the diagnosis of cosmic tendencies. He, too, focused on China. The maintenance of the principle of equality of commercial opportunity was beneficent to all mankind but even more important was an open door to ideas. China must change and if she were to become a worthy member of the family of nations, she must acquire the spiritual, as well as the material, benefits of the West. These included Christianity, one of the important influences shaping Western civilization. "If the advantage to us is great of a China open to commerce," he wrote, "the danger to us and to her is infinitely greater of a China enriched and strengthened by the material advantages we have to offer, but uncontrolled in the use of them by any clear understanding, much less any full acceptance, of the mental and moral forces which have generated, and which in large measure govern, our political and social action." It was idle, Mahan argued, to fall back on arguments "on the propriety of non-interference, or from the conventional rights of a so-called independent state to regulate its own affairs." China was no longer isolated, the process of change was already under way; it could neither be turned back nor arrested.[15]

The spirit of the times aided the cause of those groups who argued that China was important. Recent adventures into the rivalry for control of the Samoan Islands, the public excitement over the Venezuela affair, the extension of American rule to Hawaii, and the feverish campaign to liberate Cuba signified an urge to stake out claims beyond the continental boundaries and for Americans to assert themselves in world affairs. The interest in China prospered in this climate.

China, it seemed, offered the ideal place to wield influence in behalf of righteousness without sacrificing virtue. To stand in opposition to the aggressiveness of the European Powers in China, to do so by persuasion rather than by joining hands with other Powers, and to ask for no territory or sphere of influence added up to the kind of foreign policy Americans could support. And poor and helpless China aroused sympathy.

The reevaluation of China's importance to the United States coincided with what seemed the almost certain partition of China. At the close of the Sino-Japanese War of 1894–95, a victorious Japan demanded that China cede her Formosa and the highly strategic Liaotung Peninsula. Russia, with the cooperation of Germany and France, intervened and compelled Japan to withdraw her demand for Liaotung.

Russia, in turn, launched her own program, following up earlier plans for strengthening her position in the Pacific maritime provinces. In June, 1895, she was approached by France with a proposal for a joint loan to China which would enable China to pay Japan her indemnity. The loan was satisfactorily arranged. This was followed by the establishment of the Russo-Chinese Bank, an arm of the Russian Government, to finance projects in the Far East.

In April, 1896, an elderly Chinese statesman, Li Hung-chang, went to St. Petersburg to attend the coronation of Nicholas II. A group of Russian statesmen led by Count Witte, Minister for Finance, had already prepared a project whereby Russia would gain the right to build a railway from the Trans-Siberian line across northern Manchuria to Vladivostok. In turn, Russia would enter into a defensive alliance with China. Li, upon receiving a bribe of three million rubles, accepted these proposals and the two Governments signed a secret treaty on June 3, 1896. The railroad was to be constructed and operated by the Russo-Chinese Bank. Once these negotiations were completed, plans were made to secure from China the right to build a railway from the Chinese Eastern Railway southward to the Yellow Sea.

During the spring and summer of 1897, the German Government worked out plans for occupying the port of Kiaochow, for negotiating with China for a leasehold there, and for gaining Chinese recognition of a German sphere of influence in Shantung. The murder of two German missionaries in November, 1897, gave Germany a convenient excuse for the occupation of Kiaochow and the negotiations that followed, carried out under duress, gave Germany what she wanted.

The German occupation set off a heated debate in St. Petersburg as to whether Germany's action should be made the basis for demanding a warm water port either in Korea or Liaotung. Count Witte, at an important conference held on November 26, 1897, dissuaded his colleagues from taking action. Witte, an advocate of peaceful economic penetration, argued that to occupy a Korean port or Port Arthur on the Liaotung Peninsula, posed the danger of provoking Japan into seizing a port. Then, argued Witte, under the terms of the treaty of alliance with China, Russia would be obligated to go to war. The conference decision, however, was reversed within a matter of weeks by the Russian Government, and a Russian squadron moved into the harbor at Port Arthur. In March, 1898, thanks again to generous bribes to Li Hung-chang and to members of the Tsung-li Yamen, China consented to a treaty granting Russia a lease of Port Arthur and the right to build a railway southward from the Chinese Eastern through southern Manchuria.

Both Great Britain and Japan showed concern but for different reasons. The British had no serious objection to the Russian occupation of Port Arthur but they were genuinely concerned over rumors that Russia was about to press for a sphere of interest in an area where British trade was important.[16] The Japanese feared the establishment of naval bases that could serve as future jumping off places for an attack. Though deeply disturbed, they decided to postpone any action. Great Britain, seeking to counterbalance Russia, negotiated a lease of the harbor of Wei-hai-wei.

These developments gained worldwide attention and evoked heated comment from Charles Denby, the American Minister in Peking, and likewise by E. H. Conger who succeeded Denby in July, 1898.

Regular reports, written in great detail and with deep emotion as to the callousness displayed, were provided by Charles Denby. Denby singled out Germany and Russia for the harshest censure—while he expressed regret because Great Britain failed to take a strong stand in opposition. Denby related to the Secretary of State the German seizure of Kiaochow and how, when the Chinese debated how to defend themselves, the Russian Minister urged them not to oppose Germany for Russia would defend China. And then Russia used the precedent set to make equally stern demands. Regarding Russia's course, Denby wrote: "International intercourse does not contain an episode of greater moral baseness than this."[17]

Denby advised Secretary of State John Sherman in the midst of these happenings: "I content myself with saying that in my opinion an energetic protest from our Government against the dismemberment of China might have a good effect in strengthening the hands of nations like Japan and Great Britain who are freer to act in this contingency than we are."[18] In another letter Denby urged, "Our moral support should be given to Great Britain if she will do anything."[19]

When E. H. Conger arrived as Minister, he showed less emotional sympathy for the Chinese. For a brief time, he believed that the United States should counter the seizures by the other Powers by staking out her own claim. He considered the success of the Russians in securing control of railroads in North China to be highly detrimental to American interests and explained his reasons:

1'st, because it removes from American capital extremely rare
opportunities for profitable investment, and by just so much takes
from us permanent and potent channels of trade possibilities and
political influence.

There has never been a time in our political or commercial history,
when such a loss meant so much to our people.[20]

American industry, wrote Conger, had just reached the stage
when it could successfully compete. Only if Americans were free
to invest and promote trade could they offset the territorial ac-
quisitions of other strong nations. Conger believed that the traditions of the United States closed the door to territorial acquisition, but after another month's observation of the scene, he
advised the Secretary of State that occupation of Manila in the
Philippines would serve her interests in China.[21]

By November, 1898, Conger, increasingly troubled by the
situation confronting him in Peking, returned to the question
of what policy would best serve American interests. It was true,
he said, that the integrity of China could be preserved by an
alliance of a few great powers, but this raised the question as "to
what end?" He thought it not worthwhile if it meant no more
than preserving "the old China without possibility of material
development or trade progress." If economic development were
to take place, then "orientalism must effectually give way to
occidentalism." He considered the latter to be almost inevitable.
In the event that it did take place, the United States should "see
to it that as many doors are left open for us as possible, and we
ought to be ready, either by negotiation or by actual possession,
to own and control at least one good port from which we can
potently assert our rights and effectively wield our influence." [22]

Not until a year after the division of China into spheres of
influence did the United States commit itself and seek to commit
all others to the Open Door Policy. The story of how the Open
Door Notes came to be written and sent to the Governments
with important interests in China has been told many times and
needs no repetition. Alfred E. Hippisley, a Briton who had served
in China in the Imperial Maritime Customs Service for several
decades, and W. W. Rockhill, adviser to John Hay on Far Eastern
Affairs and a noted oriental scholar, shared in the drafting of the

policy. The Notes sought to have the Powers concerned subscribe
to the principle of preserving equality of commercial opportunity in China. To achieve this goal, the nations holding spheres
of interest were to agree not to charge higher harbor dues, levy
higher freight rates, or otherwise discriminate against the trade
of other nationals within their own sphere. Tariff duties were to
be the same for nationals of the country controlling the sphere
of interest as for all others.[23] They were to be collected by the
Chinese thus assuring equal treatment and providing for the
continued exercise by China of sovereignty within the spheres.

The aim, at least on the surface, was to extend the ideal of a
free market, as American a panacea as private enterprise. However, Rockhill and Hippisley had also taken a stand in support
of China's territorial integrity and independence.[24] This is apparent not only from their correspondence but from a note to
Minister Conger, written during the March following the dispatch of the Open Door Notes. On March 22, Hay wrote in
longhand to Conger concerning the Boxer disturbances. In it he
instructed Conger:

> . . . you will avail yourself of every opportunity to impress upon it
> (the Tsung-li Yamen) that this Government by the recent assur-
> ances which it has obtained from the various great Powers holding
> leased territory or spheres of influence in China, concerning free-
> dom of trade in said spheres and the maintenance therein of
> China's rights of sovereignty, has obtained thereby renewed assur-
> ance of the policy of the Treaty Powers not to interfere with the
> integrity of the Chinese Empire.[25]

The Notes did not seek to abolish spheres of influence; in fact,
they recognized and accepted the fact of spheres, but at the same
time, the aim was to reduce their importance.

The negotiations with the Powers continued throughout the
closing months of 1899. Except for Japan, the replies were evasive and qualified, and it has often been said that in pronouncing
the responses to be satisfactory, Hay engaged in bluff. In one
sense, this is true; the replies of the Powers did not constitute firm
commitments. But the question has to be asked as to the nature
of the commitment Hay sought. Hay had scarcely intended to
commit the United States to upholding China's territorial and
administrative integrity against the efforts of any one nation or

group of nations that might take steps inconsistent with this goal. Moreover, to affirm respect for another nation's territorial and administrative integrity when limited to the specific curbs named was radically different from a commitment to uphold China against all others in future crises. Such a commitment would have been far beyond the capabilities of the United States and the cost would have far outrun national interests. Given this point of view, Hay could scarcely worry about the qualified nature of the acceptances. Hay had provided a guiding principle and he drew from the various Governments sufficient assurances so that he had a lever to use in protesting against future violations. Hay knew only too well the limits of the commitment of his own Government. The American public was far from ready to support a firm position unless American lives were involved.

The outbreak of the Boxer Revolt in June, 1900, with the siege against the Foreign Legations in Peking, the slaughter of missionaries together with thousands of Chinese Christians in North China and Manchuria provided precisely the kind of occasion when Hay could count on public support. During that summer, the United States moved into the role of direct participant. American troops joined in the expedition to lift the siege of the Legations and Hay entered energetically into the negotiations to prevent the spread of the rebellion into the Yangtze Valley and to bring about a settlement that would avoid the partition of China.

Panic seized the extensive foreign settlement at Shanghai after the beginning of the siege in Peking and rumors of what each country was about to do filled the air. The nationals of each of the Powers, wrote Consul-General John Goodnow in Shanghai, pressured their Consuls to use the occasion to seize territory. One of the most disturbing stories was that the British were about to occupy the Woosung forts and the Shanghai arsenal. The British Consul told Goodnow "that the Viceroy has offered the English Government through him joint occupation of these places." Then, J. W. Ferguson, an American in the employ of the Chinese Government and adviser to the Viceroy, told Goodnow, "that the English Consul-General at that time told the Chinese authorities that the allied fleets of all nations except England had arranged to seize the Woosung forts at a given time and asked the Taotai if he did not wish the English to land and take joint control of these places in order that the other Nations might not seize them." [26]

On June 26, a most important agreement was reached between the foreign Consuls and the two Yangtze Valley Viceroys, Liu Kun-yi and Chang Chih-tung, whereby these two powerful Viceroys agreed to protect foreigners and the Consuls agreed that the troops of their Governments would take no action.[27]

On July 1, John Hay discussed this agreement with John Bassett Moore who seized the occasion to press upon the Secretary of State the advantages to be gained by the United States announcing "that its guiding principle was the preservation of the independence and territorial integrity of the Chinese Empire, and to endeavor to secure the express assent of the Powers to it." When Hay stated that he thought Russia would be opposed, Moore met the objection by the argument that Russia would probably go along "since the refusal to give it would be equivalent to an avowal of a sinister purpose which at the moment she probably would wish not to exhibit; . . . ."

Moore pointed to "the immediate interest that we have in the fate of China in consequence of holding the Philippines." "If Russia, or Russia and powers in alliance with her, held China," he argued, "we should be at their mercy in the Philippines." "Besides," Moore noted in his memorandum of the conversation, "I argued that the idea of supporting the independence and integrity of China would accord with the sentiments of our people; that it was this principle of helping other nations to maintain their independence and integrity that had made the Monroe Doctrine so popular amongst them; . . . ."

Hay told Moore that the President and the Attorney General "had been inclined to favor the policy of seizing a port in China, and getting a foothold there, as other powers had done, but that he himself, though he would like to have a port, as a naval station, thought it would be unfortunate to take such a step, particularly at the present time." Moore advised Hay that he believed such a step would be "very unacceptable to our people and would have an unfortunate effect on public sentiment, as the cry of 'land grabbing' would at once be raised; . . . ."

Moore added an interesting observation concerning the attitude of some Americans toward China. These people, he said, "mostly students and men unfamiliar with practical affairs, had conceived that it would be a good thing if the Powers would take China under their tutelage, and reorganize and transform her; . . . ." Moore thought this ignored the size of China's population and her ancient and persistent civilization. It was, he said, "a fantastic conception based on erroneous principles." [28]

The tenseness continued and Viceroy Liu appealed to Goodnow who telegraphed John Hay: "Viceroy urges President take leading part says only hope China through settlement by America pushing aside selfish schemes." [29] This telegram was received at 1:30 P.M. on July 3. On that same day, Hay sent his Circular Note to the Powers stating that it was the policy of the United States to bring about "permanent safety and peace to China" and to support her territorial and administrative integrity. It is not possible to determine whether Viceroy Liu's appeal inspired the Secretary of State to appeal to the Powers or whether the timing was coincidental. The Circular Note testified to American goodwill and Hay's efforts to prevent dismemberment.

On August 20, the Allied Military Expedition reached Peking and lifted the siege, but great difficulties remained. The Imperial Court fled westward, the Boxers remained at large, and there was general fear that unless order were restored, the revolt might spread southward. Conger called for a quick settlement. "If it is not done speedily," he warned Hay, "the partition of China is inevitable." "Military occupation by so many powers," he telegraphed, "is creating irreparable devastation, and bringing terrible punishment upon innocent people; and if long continued, will arouse such hatred among the people as to render the situation difficult, and induce uprising against all foreigners in peaceable provinces." [30]

Rockhill, who had recently been appointed Special Commissioner to China, arrived in Peking shortly after the lifting of the siege. His reports told of the bad behavior of many of the foreign troops, the hunting down of innocent peasants seeking to harvest the grain, and at Tientsin, a "disposition of all parties to seize for their use . . . every site, property, or belonging which pleased their fancy or tempted their cupidity." [31] Between Tientsin and

Peking, the villages were "one mass of ruins, some now held by detachments of foreign troops; others completely deserted." Rockhill joined with Conger in urging "the imperative necessity of maintaining the present force of troops in Peking until after the signing of at least the preliminaries of peace" if the Chinese were to be convinced of the necessity of negotiating.[32]

During his stay in Peking, Rockhill called on Prince Ch'ing who was already urging the Court to return to Peking. The Prince expressed his gratification for Hay's Circular Note of July 3.[33] Rockhill also called on Sir Robert Hart who interpreted the Boxer movement "as a national and patriotic one for freeing China of the foreigners to whom, rightly or wrongly, it attributed all the country's misfortunes during the last half century." In prophetic words, as reported by Rockhill, Hart warned: "Though crushed at present, he feared that unless the Powers would agree to treat the question in a conciliatory spirit which would tend to establish cordial relations with China—a state which had never existed in the past—it might someday come to life again when the world might have to face an armed China, not a rabble carrying spears and tridents." [34]

Because of the concern that the Boxer disturbances might erupt in a new form in the Yangtze Valley, Rockhill went from Peking down to Shanghai and then to Nanking and Wuchang. At Nanking, he called on Viceroy Liu and thanked him for his statesmanship in maintaining peace and order. In turn, Liu replied that "it was particularly pleasant to him to protect American interests as he had always felt a strong inclination towards our country whose policy in China had always been, and was especially now, friendly and disinterested." Liu agreed on the importance of the Emperor returning to Peking and entering negotiations but he felt unable to urge his return for reasons Rockhill deemed adequate.[35] Rockhill then called on Viceroy Chang Chih-tung. He, too, thought it impossible to arrange immediately for the Emperor's return to Peking and suggested instead that the Powers should accept as evidence of the Emperor's willingness and ability to restore order his cutting himself off from the advisers who had supported the Boxers. He did think that it was possible to induce the Emperor to demonstrate that he was a free agent. Rockhill showed sympathy and understanding for the two Viceroys who faced a dangerous situation owing to the recent appointment of antiforeign officials in their provinces, the drain on their treasuries to support the Court, and the bad harvests and prostration of trade.[36] Both Viceroys promised that they would continue to preserve peace and order as long as it was within their power to do so.

Early in September, at his summer home in New Hampshire, John Hay pondered the question of what role the United States should play in the months ahead. Conger and Rockhill both urged that American troops should not be withdrawn. Their presence was necessary if the Chinese were to agree to the kind of a settlement these two men envisaged. However, Hay at first preferred to reduce the number of these troops to a small police force and to withdraw them from Peking. This would make it easier for the Emperor to return, and even the presence of a small number of troops would be sufficient "to uphold the Emperor's hand in dealing out justice." [37]

But Hay was clearly groping for answers, and he wrote to Adee:

> The dilemma is clear enough. We want to get out at the earliest possible moment. We do not want to have the appearance of being forced out, or frightened out, and we must not lose our proper influence in the final arrangement. If we leave Germany and England in Peking, and retire with Russia, who has unquestionably made her bargain already with China, we will not only *seem* to have been beaten, but we run a serious risk of being *really* frozen out. Germany and England will feel resentful and will take no care of our interests, and Russia will see us out without winking. You have, it seems, grave suspicion of the attitude of Japan. There is, therefore, not a single power we can rely on, for our policy of abstention from plunder and the Open Door.[38]

To this Hay added the observation that China would not commit herself to resisting those powers bent on territorial seizure and economic arrangements detrimental to Chinese control. "China," wrote Hay, "will say to us as she said last year, 'We are not free agents. We are not able without the permission of the other powers, to fulfil any engagements we might make with you.' " [39]

This chilling analysis did not induce paralysis and retreat.

Hay decided in favor of continued participation with the hope of having some modest influence on the outcome of the negotiations in Peking. However, he did not share the lighthearted confidence of those groups, motivated either by missionary zeal or by hope of commercial gain, who conveniently ignored the political realities.

In his brief to Conger for the Conference of Ministers proceeding in Peking, Hay stated the long-term aim of his Government. The United States, he wrote, sought: "Increased intercourse with the Chinese Empire under conditions no less beneficial to China than to foreign nations, so as to perpetuate peace and order by building up the prosperity of China." [40] The rest of Hay's instructions concerned more immediate goals regarding the terms of the Boxer settlement. The modesty of Hay's expectations needs to be underlined. His commitments were equally modest.

The long drawn out negotiations in Peking were soon under way and almost at once John Hay found two of his proposals unacceptable to the other Powers. The first of these called for a lump sum indemnity, a step considered necessary to prevent extravagant demands on China and the probable settlement of the question by China paying not in money but in territory. The second proposal asked that there be incorporated in the preamble to the prospective agreement, a new affirmation by each of the Powers of their respect for China's territorial and administrative integrity and equality of commercial opportunity. Conger found most of his colleagues strongly opposed to such a declaration "which they held had been so often made by their respective Governments that there was no necessity of repeating it again." [41] Rockhill explained the situation to Hay and added that while it was true that most of the Powers had given expression to the views supported by him, it would be useful to incorporate these principles because "they have never been embodied in a treaty or convention with China." [42] To this Hay responded: "In reply I have to say that the Department does not expect impossibilities, and it thinks that the incorporation of such declaration, in the places suggested by you, would be of great advantage." [43]

The big question by the close of the year 1900 concerned Russia, and both Conger and Rockhill had warned Hay that she would probably take over Manchuria and perhaps North China. "Altogether, Russia is having, and will in all probability continue to have, everything her own way in this part of the world," Rockhill wrote.[44] He thought Japan and Russia might well arrive at an agreement as to what each should have.[45]

What would Russia's taking over of Manchuria mean to the United States? The coauthor of the Open Door Notes, Rockhill, observed: "Fortunately, she will not be for many years to come a serious competitor for the trade of Eastern Asia and so, if our interests out here are purely commercial—which I do not, however, think they are, we may still confidently expect our China trade to go on increasing." [46]

The reports from China in January and February of 1901 did not simplify the problems Hay faced. Rather they must have confirmed his feeling that not much could be accomplished by the United States. Both Conger and Rockhill condemned the weakness of the diplomats who were participating in the negotiations. "Every day I am more convinced of the uniform mediocrity of the Dipl. corps here—not a man rises, even a little, above the others . . .," wrote Rockhill.[47]

At times the two American diplomats deplored the harsh demands put forth, but they also bemoaned the lack of firmness in confronting the Chinese. Rockhill reported that the Chinese were simply marking time because they "have simply to wait to see every demand scaled down by the Powers." [48] He was also upset that the Chinese had learned of the proposed scheme of evacuation of Peking before they agreed to constructive reforms.

Rockhill further regretted that the Ministers indicated a willingness to raise tariff duties so that China would be better able to pay the indemnity. "Putting aside the fact that such a concession on the part of the Powers at the present time would undoubtedly be interpreted by the Chinese as a great victory, it seems to me," he wrote, "that the present time is an excellent moment to coerce China to develop her own resources, and that they should be drawn upon rather than any others." [49] Rockhill favored pushing the Chinese into promoting mining and also a withdrawal of subsidies to the Manchus. He noted: "I feel convinced this source of revenue should be put to better use than to maintain in idleness a couple of millions of drones." [50]

Rockhill's observations on the Chinese contributed nothing towards promoting any hope that the United States could rely on them to stand firm in the defense of their own interests if the United States supported them. He wrote to Hay of the "absolutely rotten official class" and predicted, "They will do nothing." [51]

The altruistic side of the American relationship to China took on mean dimensions as seen from Peking. Missionaries had suffered at the hands of the Boxers; their converts had suffered infinitely more. To affirm their devotion to those who had experienced brutality because they remained loyal to the foreign religious faith, missionaries worked feverishly to right the wrongs their disciples suffered. So it appeared to the missionaries, but to Rockhill in Peking their efforts were cast in a different light. He reported to Hay how missionaries presented "lists of persons they wish put to death, the evidence of these officials guilt being furnished them by native Christians." "It is extraordinary," he wrote, "to see such grave responsibility assumed with such light-heartedness." [52]

What, then, was the U.S. policy? What were its aims as of January, 1901? The previous June, Hay had instructed Conger:

> We have no policy in China except to protect with energy American interests, and especially American citizens and the legation. There must be nothing done which would commit us to future action inconsistent with your standing instructions. There must be no alliances. [53]

He could have written the same in January, 1901, after the turbulence of the Boxers, the participation of an American expeditionary force in lifting the siege of the Legations in Peking, and the continued presence of that force for political reasons. The policy was as lean of commitments as ever. There was the irreducible minimum, the upholding of treaty rights, especially the protection of American lives. There was the aim of fostering an economically developed China, but this was accepted as remote and not an aim to be implemented at once by the coercion of China into ways of reform. There was likewise the aim of maintaining a voice in Chinese affairs, an implied insistence that the United States was a Pacific Power whose interests could not be ignored by the European nations.

Policy had not changed. Yet things were not the same. The experience of involvement left little, if any, disillusionment among casual observers, and they believed that they had wielded an influence for good. The diplomatic pronouncement of July 3 had also made an impact. The United States had boldly opposed those who would have partitioned China. So while policy had not changed, the public myth that the United States stood for a strong policy in China was established.

NOTES

1. U.S., *Congressional Record,* 55th Congress, 2nd Session, 1898, XXXI, Part 6, 5906.
2. U.S., Bureau of the Census, *Statistical Abstract of the United States: 1898* (Washington: U.S. Government Printing Office, 1898), p. 282.
3. U.S., Bureau of the Census, *Statistical Abstract of the United States: 1900* (Washington: U.S. Government Printing Office, 1900), p. 323.
4. *The Foreign Commerce and Navigation of the United States for the Year Ending June 30, 1910* (Washington: U.S. Government Printing Office, 1910), p. 544.
5. *Ibid.,* p. 770.
6. *A Geography and Atlas of Protestant Missions,* II, *Statistics and Atlas* by Harlan P. Beach (New York: Student Volunteer Movement for Foreign Missions, 1903), 23.
7. Sherwood Eddy, *Pathfinders of the World Missionary Crusade* (New York: Abingdon-Cokesbury Press, 1945), p. 50.
8. Arthur H. Smith, *Chinese Characteristics* (New York: Fleming H. Revell Co., 1894), pp. 136–137.
9. John L. Nevius, *China and the Chinese: A General Description of the Country and Its Inhabitants; Its Civilization and Form of Government; Its Religious and Social Institutions; Its Intercourse with other Nations; and Its Present Condition and Prospects* (Chicago: Missionary Campaign Library Number Two, 1882), pp. 289–290.
10. *The Student Missionary Appeal: Addresses at the Third International Convention of the Student Volunteer Movement for Foreign Missions* (New York: Student Volunteer Movement for Foreign Missions, 1898), p. 328.
11. F. F. Ellinwood, "The Religions of China," *The Missionary Review of the World,* XIII (February, 1890), 148.
12. James W. Bashford, *China: An Interpretation* (New York: The Abingdon Press, 1916), p. 195.
13. Fletcher S. Brockman, *I Discover the Orient* (New York: Harper and Brothers, 1935), pp. 14–15.
14. Brooks Adams, *America's Economic Supremacy* (New York: The Macmillan Company, 1900). This is a brief summary of the argument of the book as a whole.

15. Alfred Thayer Mahan, "Effects of Asiatic Conditions Upon International Policies," *North American Review*, CLXX (November, 1900), 609–626.

16. Andrew Malozemoff, *Russian Far Eastern Policy 1881–1904: With Special Emphasis on the Causes of the Russo–Japanese War* (Berkeley: University of California Press, 1958), pp. 105–106.

17. Denby to Secretary of State John Sherman, March 19, 1898, Department of State Archives.

18. *Ibid.*, March 8, 1898.

19. *Ibid.*, March 19, 1898.

20. Conger to Secretary of State William R. Day, July 31, 1898.

21. *Ibid.*, August 26, 1898.

22. Conger to Secretary of State John Hay, November 3, 1898, Department of State Archives.

23. *See* A. Whitney Griswold, *The Far Eastern Policy of the United States* (New York: Harcourt, Brace and Company, 1938), pp. 72–78 and the author's *Open Door Diplomat: The Life of W. W. Rockhill* (Urbana: University of Illinois Press, 1952), pp. 29–33.

24. Varg, *Open Door Diplomat*, p. 33.

25. Hay to Conger, March 22, 1900, Department of State Archives.

26. Goodnow to Assistant Secretary of State T. W. Cridler, June 29, 1900, Department of State Archives.

27. Chester Tan, *The Boxer Catastrophe* (New York: Columbia University Press, 1955), pp. 80–82.

28. John Bassett Moore's memorandum of conversation with Secretary of State John Hay, July 1, 1900, Moore Papers, Library of Congress.

29. Goodnow to Hay, July 3, 1900, Department of State Archives.

30. Conger to Hay, September 6, 1900, Department of State Archives.

31. Rockhill to Hay, October 1, 1900, Department of State Archives.

32. *Ibid.*, September 1, 1900.

33. *Ibid.*, October 1, 1900.

34. *Ibid.*, October 25, 1900.

35. *Ibid.*

36. *Ibid.*, December 10, 1900.

37. Hay to Alvey A. Adee, September 14, 1900, Hay Papers, Library of Congress.

38. *Ibid.*

39. *Ibid.*

40. Hay to Conger, December 29, 1900.

41. *Ibid.*

42. *Ibid.*

43. Hay to Rockhill, February 2, 1901.

44. Rockhill to Hay, January 29, 1901, Hay Papers.

45. *Ibid.*, January 9, 1901.

46. *Ibid.*, January 29, 1901.

47. Rockhill to Hay, February 4, 1901, Hay Papers.

48. *Ibid.*

49. *Ibid.*
50. *Ibid.*
51. *Ibid.*, January 29, 1901.
52. *Ibid.*, February 4, 1901.
53. Hay to Conger, June 10, 1900, Department of State Archives.

CHAPTER III

THE MYTH OF THE CHINA MARKET

JOHN HAY won public acclaim for his Open Door Notes and his reaffirmation of this policy in the July 3 Circular Note. At the close of the Boxer Revolt, the public expected him to bring about a settlement consistent with the principles he enunciated. There was no turning back; the popularity of his stance deprived Hay of freedom to retreat.

The thrust into Asia owed much to that segment of the business community interested in the China market and to the publicists who linked prosperity with sales to China's four hundred million customers. The ardent proponents talked about the future rather than the present. Exports to China had increased sufficiently to provide a basis for their argument and those who wrote about the future never failed to cite statistics that supported their cause. Exports of cotton goods had increased dramatically, and most of these went to North China and southern Manchuria, the area threatened by Russian expansion. But there, sales, never more than a miniscule portion of total American exports, became the indices for measuring the potential of the China market for manufactured goods.

From the middle of the 1890's to 1906, exports to China showed only a modest rate of growth but were sufficient to maintain faith in the earlier predictions. No one challenged this optimistic view. However, from 1906 to the Chinese Revolution of 1911, when annual export figures moved both up and down, there were some second thoughts. Declines were readily explained as caused by temporary phenomena. In 1906, the unsettling effects of the Russo-Japanese War and the piling up of supplies in warehouses during the hostilities received much attention. In the next few years, the difficulties were explained as due to the instability of the Chinese currency. Both, unquestionably, did hamper trade but conditions in China of a more permanent character were of greater importance.

In this period, too, it became apparent that there was reason to question the generally accepted assumption that the nations establishing leaseholds and spheres of influence would utilize them to favor their own exporters. Therefore, these should be opposed as hostile to the commercial interests of the United States. Other Governments did favor their own nationals, but in some cases, American sales increased within the spheres of influence due to the economic development fostered by the controlling nation. Sales of railroad equipment to Japan's South Manchuria Railway offered the best illustration.

The facts notwithstanding, the prospect of a large market for manufactured goods lost but little of its luster prior to the Chinese Revolution. This continued to serve as one of the major reasons for the United States to make its influence felt in Chinese affairs. But there is also cause for reflection as to the real meaning of the repeated reliance of the Department of State on the commercial argument whenever it confronted a development in the China crucible that it found objectionable. It was undoubtedly convenient to object to a particular move on the part of other nations on the ground that it would violate the rights of American business to an equality of commercial opportunity, but the argument served more than business interests. It provided a suitable basis for those responsible for the conduct of foreign relations to assert an interest and to convey to other Powers that the United States was an interested party. Not until 1909, when Philander Knox became Secretary of State, did the United States make a determined effort to initiate arrangements which would enlarge the prospects of American business. Even then, the political aim seems to have been as important as the commercial. However, these reflections pertain only to the thinking of statesmen. A segment of the business community entertained the prospect of a growing market in China and it was interested in business, not the political future of East Asia.

The most elementary facts contradicted the dream that China would, before long, provide a large market. The first of these was that only a small part of China, the coastal cities and a few ports on the rivers, was open to trade. In 1899, Rounseville Wildman, the U.S. Consul-General in Hongkong, wrote:

> Another great point that American exporters overlook is that 99 percent of China is still closed to the world. When the magazine writer refers in glowing terms to the 400,000,000 inhabitants of China, he forgets that 350,000,000 are a dead letter so far as commerce is concerned.[1]

Burlingame Johnson, the Consul in Amoy, in 1901, called for treaty revisions which would permit businessmen to reside in the interior. Such action, he believed, would open the markets as far away "as 150 to 200 miles . . . whereas now even kerosene and flour seldom get further than fifty miles from open ports and few other goods that far." [2]

The lack of a transportation system restricted the influx of western goods. Except for river traffic, transport was almost nonexistent. The Grand Canal, which, in the time of Marco Polo, carried large vessels over a six hundred and fifty mile stretch between Peking and Hangchow, was in disrepair and small junks now navigated it with difficulty. Of the roads, the U.S. Consul in Shanghai in 1895 reported:

> Their condition is such that passage over them is virtually stopped as the holes and ruts that deface them force travelers to desert them for the tracks by the sides, although these in wet weather are but quagmires, and in dry weather, several inches in dust.[3]

A survey of the roads in 1890 by the China branch of the Royal Asiatic Society led to this conclusion:

> Probably no country in the world, certainly none aiming at civilization even of the most rudimentary nature, has paid so little attention to roads and means of communication as had the Chinese empire; and it may be remarked at the outset that no road in the European acceptance of the term, as an artificially constructed viaduct, laid out with engineering skill even of the crudest description, exists from one end of China to the other.[4]

Given these conditions, only a small part of the country was accessible to foreign goods.

Another formidable barrier stood in the way. Western goods fitted neither ancient Chinese preferences nor Chinese pocketbooks. Flour, cotton goods, kerosene and lumber jibed with the native consumer habits and did find a growing market, but the great variety of western goods ran counter to long-established ways of work and customs. In 1906, James L. Rodgers, the Consul-General in Shanghai, wrote: "It is perhaps needless to call attention to the antiquity of Chinese methods and habits, to the fact that traders have for centuries been trying to introduce new things, and that beyond some modern devices for using and making the necessities of life, one sees very few inroads upon established customs." [5] Rodgers stated that the Chinese did buy foreign oil, flour, leather, lamps, clocks and some food stuffs, but, he warned, "it does not follow that there is a market for a foreign shoe, for an agricultural implement, for machinery of various kinds and for the infinite variety of manufactured goods which distinguish the industry of the United States, Great Britain, and Germany." A certain Occidental, Rodgers reported, had written home that there was a great market for windmills. Such an opinion ignored the fact that the Chinese had been raising water from one level to another by means of pumps and water wheels long before the Christian era began and they were not likely to change their methods. Even more important than the reluctance to change, he declared, was the fact that "a windmill would cost many rice crops, or perhaps the savings of a lifetime. . . ."

Rodgers, after an examination of the markets in the Chinese cities near Shanghai, noted that there were few foreign products and "you will hunt for a day before you will find in this section of China an agricultural implement of foreign make."[6] He concluded: "Numberless instances might be cited to show how limited a Chinese market is for things which encroach upon their customs or which will supplant the articles handed down from generation to generation. . . ." In conclusion, he offered these words: "And all this is written not to discourage but to place that which is conceived to be plain truth before the minds of those who nowadays read in the newspapers glowing prophecies about the oriental trade, who then remember that there are said to be four hundred million Chinese and who are straightway moved to attempt an export business to China. . . ." Given the "present scheme of civilization" whereby the Chinese "are practically sufficient unto themselves," he warned, "China, even under the reformation now beginning, will take at first only in a small way of those things she does not seem to need. . . ."[7]

The poverty of the Chinese constituted a further obstacle. When the Department of State, in 1898, instructed Consuls throughout the world to report on the possible outlets for the surplus product of soap manufacturers, E. T. Williams, then Vice-Consul-General in Shanghai, wrote:

> The people of China are extremely poor. Their wages are paid in copper cash, one of which equals one-twentieth of a cent. One hundred to one hundred and fifty of these cash, that is, from five to seven and a half cents, form the average daily wage of the ordinary working man. It is evident that such an article as soap, which from the Chinese point of view, is an article of luxury rather than necessity, however, much desired, can be purchased only when furnished at a very low price.[8]

As Gerald Winfield was to put it five decades later in his book *China: the Land and the People,* the poverty that prevailed had as its symbol the family pig. Other livestock was extremely rare because feeding entailed a loss of nutritional elements, but the pig, living in the family latrine, required almost no feeding.

Other countries emerging from an almost wholly agricultural economy turned natural resources and an abundant supply of cheap labor into assets through rapid industrialization. Japan is a noteworthy example. In China, the change was slow. The Central Government lacked the necessary revenue to foster industry with any degree of rapidity and Chinese social values, especially the tradition of investing any surplus savings in land, handicapped the development of industry. The custom of "squeeze," nepotism, and the use of government-owned enterprises for personal political ends likewise stood in the way of economic development.

Another deterrent to a market for American goods was the rapid development after 1894 of an unfavorable trade balance. Exports to China did increase but exports from China did not. A study of China's long-term trade developments made by the Imperial Maritime Customs Service in 1904 showed that China's imports had increased until they were a third greater than exports. Indemnities incurred as a result of the war with Japan and the Boxer Revolt had necessitated foreign loans thereby increasing the outflow of gold. These foreign loans, in 1904, called for payments upwards of forty-five million haikwan taels a year.[9]

Within this market, so circumscribed by inaccessibility to the interior, by aversion to western style products, by poverty, and by an unfavorable balance of international payments, a dog-eat-dog fight for sales and contracts raged. Germany, Great Britain, France, Russia, and Japan were more dependent upon foreign markets than the United States; the Governments of these nations gave their business enterprises greater support than did the United States, and, most important, the business enterprises of these countries demonstrated greater energy and initiative in China. Consequently, American companies found the going rough.

The Standard Oil Company, oriented to foreign markets by long experience and by the fact that since the 1860's more than half of its major product, kerosene, was exported, eyed the Far East. As early as 1882, the company sent William Herbert Libby to explore possible markets in that part of the world. He made a careful study of the China situation and more particularly of the barriers to greater sales of kerosene. Beginning in 1890, Standard Oil, anxious to expand sales, departed from the practice of selling to merchants on the Atlantic Seaboard who then handled sales in China. Under the new system, it distributed its products through its British affiliate, the Anglo-American Oil Company.[10] In the next two decades, sales increased but Standard Oil's hopes of dominating the market never came even close to realization. Russian oil enjoyed the advantages of lower production costs, shorter transportation routes, and benefited by the tariffs levied on value as opposed to volume.[11] The competition of the Dutch operating out of the East Indies also cut seriously into Standard Oil's sales in China. Standard Oil, more than any other American company, adopted a system of distribution and sales that was efficient and well suited to success in China, but although sales became important, the competition of the Russians and the Dutch was so effective that, in the words of the historians of the company, its "efforts in the Far East proved relatively ineffectual."[12]

These barriers to trade, although not readily surmountable,

sometimes appeared minor in comparison to inveterate Chinese hostility toward the foreigner. Indeed, the one characteristic quality of the Chinese in relations with the outside world—whether political, economic, or religious—was an intractable opposition. The missionaries, more often exposed to antagonism because their efforts touched upon matters subject to deep emotional response and because they were often in the interior, were the most frequent targets of antiforeign disturbances. Business and government representatives enjoyed the protection of treaty ports, but they could not be protected from the Chinese aversion to them that found expression in delayed negotiations, the placing of obstacles in the way of land purchases, and the playing of one foreigner against another.

Samuel F. Gracey, the Consul in Foochow, reported that after fifteen years of careful study of all ranks of Chinese officials "and all grades of Chinese, from the above-named, to the coolie class, I am persuaded that, speaking broadly, all are unfavorable to foreigners."[13] Gracey concluded that they were convinced of the superiority of their own way of doing things and they resented the intrusion of the foreigner. The official classes "resent the coming into the country of these meddlesome foreigners. They find the ground slipping from under them by the impact with Western civilization, which is forcing upon them reforms, the trend of which is all toward great changes in their cherished beliefs, customs, learnings, and methods; and they cannot see whereunto all this is leading them," wrote Gracey. The literate and gentry, he added, "would only be too happy to sweep them all out of the empire."[14]

At times, the hostility toward the foreigner became particularly pronounced. The early 1890's, 1900, and the period immediately following the Russo-Japanese War saw pronounced antagonism. In February, 1906, the U.S. Consul in Hankow reported: "It would almost seem as though there was a concerted plan to do nothing the foreigner wants, but as far as possible to place every conceivable obstacle in the way of securing the rights pledged him under the treaty. . . ."[15] In June, he reported that there was a quiet but deep hostility toward all foreigners among the seven to ten thousand coolies employed by the shipping interests and tea factories in Hankow. "They are like wolves," he wrote, "one will slink away but a number of them will attack with their carrying sticks."[16]

The Government in Peking, bending before superior force, signed treaties that seemingly opened China to western business, but the Chinese illustrated the genius of the human being to resist by indirect methods. Foreign diplomats railed against this trait as a perversity peculiar to the Chinese. Samuel Gracey in Foochow negotiated for six months with the Viceroy and the Foreign Board for the purchase of land for the use of the Standard Oil Company. "They have shown constant purpose to defeat us by presenting unusual obstacles," he reported.[17] The latest device was to insist on the sellers appearing at the yamen. "It is well-known, that in many parts of the Empire, when sellers of land were required to go to the yamens, they were not only unmercifully squeezed, but in many cases were beaten, for selling to foreigners, and it became so common that no persons could be found to sell to foreigners, thus defeating treaty provision," Gracey informed the Department of State.[18] Given this marvelous exhibition of Chinese recalcitrance, even the most formidable advocates of American economic expansion inevitably had to recede.

At times the resistance of the Chinese to foreign control made the situation seem futile to those bent on opening up China to trade and development. No representative of the United States put the problem as tersely as E. H. Conger. It was, he said, a question of two choices. China could be left to herself and allowed "to proceed alone and in the same way that she has for thousands of years, with her inexhaustible resources of material and trade still undeveloped, or her mines must be opened and her railways built and trade developed by foreigners."[19] In the latter case, there would be stubborn opposition "which the Chinese government will be unable to promptly and satisfactorily suppress. . . ." He saw this as so formidable a threat to the interests of western nations that he was led to ask: "It is true the integrity of China can easily be preserved by an alliance of a few of the great powers, but to what end?"[20]

Turning our attention to a second major aspect of the problem, the willingness of the Government in Washington to lend assistance to American business, we find that the support was usually little more than an expression of goodwill. Beginning in the late 1880's, the Department of Commerce and the Department of State were vigorous in asking their officers for reports on commercial opportunities for many different types of manufactured goods. Bulletins including the reports were issued in great numbers.

Both Denby and Conger believed that the investment of American capital would spur the sale of American goods and they therefore supported their fellow countrymen when they presented proposals. In April, 1898, Denby reported to Secretary of State Sherman that he had "devoted a great deal of time and labor to the promotion of railroad projects" presented by his countrymen.[21] His successor, E. H. Conger, later in the same year wrote: "So long as I am at this legation, its aid will be cheerfully and actively given along these lines so far as is wise and proper; but experience has long since proven that neither legislation nor official aid can take the place of business enterprise in business affairs."[22] It was also true "that one of the chief elements of foreign potency, is the leverage obtained from actual occupation or ownership of territory." This was Conger's observation in August of 1898.[23] During the next few years, the reverse was also true on occasion. Americans received some advantage because their schemes were considered to be free of political ambitions. In the period 1894 to 1906, Washington, through its representative in Peking, struck the boldest pose at the time that the Chinese Government cancelled the contract of the American China Development Company for building the railroad from Hankow to Canton. The cancellation led to sharp diplomatic notes and the Minister, W. W. Rockhill, questioned the chief of China's Foreign Office in a most peremptory tone.[24]

However, the promotion of economic interests was generally the function of the Consular Service rather than the Legation in Peking. If the degree of government support of the Consular Service is a fair measure of how seriously Washington took the promotion of interests in China, the conclusion can only be that interest approximated apathy. For years, the Consul-General in Shanghai protested that the American consular offices in that city were not only inadequate but reflected unfavorably upon the United States. As late as 1905, Consul-General Rodgers declared that they were the poorest of any foreign nation except Portugal.

The inadequacy of consular offices had its parallel in a very small staff. Rodgers compared the failure to provide an adequate group of American officers with the elaborate efforts of Great Britain, Germany, France and Japan. In September, 1905, he reported:

They know for instance that Great Britain has a force of Englishmen in the various departments of its representation; that Germany has not only a large number here, but also has men traveling on trade matters; that France is likewise provided and that Japan is represented elsewhere. They know that absolute count will show that in Shanghai where the United States has one employee, Great Britain and Germany have six, France about four and Japan counting only those in evidence, three.[25]

All of the districts found reason to complain but no one demonstrated greater impatience than Edward Bedloe who was appointed Consul in Canton in the latter part of 1897. On arrival, he found the offices so inadequately furnished that he carried on business from his hotel room. When facing the necessity of giving a reception in the offices for Chinese officials and other Consuls, he borrowed furnishings from several friendly parties.[26]

The importance of the Canton district seemed to justify better quarters and a more adequate staff. Eighty million people lived in the area. Some seven cities had been made into treaty ports in 1897 and both the British and Germans had an official at each. Consul Bedloe was the only officer representing the United States. When he first took over, he had no Vice-Consul or clerk. During his first several months he employed a clerk and paid him out of his own pocket. A Vice-Consul was appointed late in 1898 after a missionary group petitioned the Department of State.[27] The inadequacy of staff, particularly the absence of Consuls in the interior, meant there was no official to protest against a variety of types of interference with shipments of American goods or to promote American commercial interests.

The U.S. Consulate in Amoy typified the general neglect and apathy. In the early 1890's Edward Bedloe, previous to his transfer to Canton, occupied the office. A German resident served for several months after Bedloe was transferred. Then Delaware Kemper took over. In June, 1897, Burlingame Johnson, an energetic young man from Colorado, replaced Kemper. Johnson immediately reported to the Department of State "that the condition in which the work of the office has been found is very unsatisfactory." The "property," he declared, "is in a most dilapidated condition." He added: "The verandas are falling, posts have rotted off, plastings (sic!) falling, and the roof needs thorough repairs."[28] An official reading the letter noted: "He may have the flagstaff painted at once." Within a year seventeen hundred dollars were spent on renovations.

The work of the Amoy Consulate harmonized with the dismal surroundings. Burlingame Johnson informed the Department of State: "Notwithstanding this I find that absolutely no attention was given to the opening for American products by my predecessor and that for three years there has not been a single trade report to the Department calling attention of exporters to existing conditions."[29] Johnson's initial enthusiasm found expression in a detailed report on missionary work, praising its philanthropic aspects and as an activity that opened the door to commerce, but his efforts in behalf of trade do not appear to have measured up to his own high hopes.

In April, 1906, the Consul in Hankow, William Martin, complained "that all the force in this office at present, capable of doing clerical work, consists of Mr. W. B. Hull, Student Interpreter, Mr. Kong Chen-ren, the Chinese writer and myself."[30] He asked for a stenographer and a typewriter. He based his request on the sharp increase of Standard Oil's business but acknowledged that his plea had a more important basis, the great numbers of missionaries scattered over the district and the voluminous correspondence carried on with them.[31] Samuel Gracey, after many years of service, in 1902, requested restoration of his salary to what it was previously, namely, thirty-five hundred dollars. John Fowler, a veteran officer stationed in Chefoo, one of the more important posts from the point of view of sale of cotton goods, received a raise to thirty-five hundred dollars in 1905. He noted: ". . . it is the smallest salary any professional Consul or Vice-Consul is receiving at this port, and all of my colleagues in course of time will retire on a pension larger than the salary of $3500."[32] Fowler, a short time later, protested that his allowance of $1775 for contingent expenses fell far short of the average annual $3209.85 contingency expenses of the previous five years. He met the difference by dipping into his own pocket.[33]

Of course, this penurious policy resulted in a rapid turnover of personnel and in much incompetence. The interest in foreign markets led to agitation for reform, but there was long delay because appointments to foreign service assignments were an important source of patronage for members of Congress. Not until 1906 did Congress provide for improvements. In a final speech in the House of Representatives supporting the bill, Robert Adams, of Pennsylvania, cited the fact that for "sixteen years efforts have been made to secure the proposed legislation." "The new legislation," he agreed, "will go a long way in the movement that is now occupying the time of our merchants for the enlargement of our foreign commerce, for these are our advance pickets, sent throughout the world to furnish the merchants the necessary information to enlarge their business abroad."[34]

The new law establishing five categories of consular posts based on estimates of the commercial importance of the foreign city did indicate a degree of serious purpose concerning China. Shanghai and Hongkong were placed in the second category, Tientsin and Canton in the fourth and Amoy and Fuchow in the fifth among the Consul-General posts.

The improved Consular Service reflected the Government's increasing awareness of the importance of foreign trade. The importance of export markets in the eyes of Washington is also evidenced in the strong support given to economic interests in Cuba, Santo Domingo, and the Philippines after the war with Spain. The building of the Panama Canal was likewise, in part, an extending of the helping hand of government to commercial interests. Others have discussed the role of economic considerations in the move of the Taft Administration to neutralize the railroads of Manchuria. These were important but compared to the actions of some other Governments, Washington scarcely played the game in a daring manner.

We are here dealing with the market for goods rather than for investment, but the first cannot be treated without some reference to the other. The lack of investments, especially in railroads, was quite correctly viewed by contemporaries as one of the reasons why the sale of American goods was not greater.

The situation as it had developed in 1909 was well described by C. S. Donaldson, Chief of the Consular Division of the Bureau of Manufactures. He explained how the bankers of Germany, France and Great Britain, with government support, established banking houses in China, South America and elsewhere and then "turned all the trade possible to their nationals."[35] Against these "tripartite combinations of government, banker and the manufacturing exporter, the American seeking trade abroad has contended single-handed." The United States, he said, was just now beginning to lend a hand, and he cited the work of individual diplomatic representatives, the effect of the Government handling the customs revenues of the Dominican Republic, and the participation of the Department of State in refunding the twenty-million-dollar debts of Costa Rica and Honduras. The Bureau of Manufactures was now providing useful information to exporters and officials were likewise to be credited with "useful achievements." The author praised the Consuls. Yet, while a new energy was making itself felt, Donaldson warned: "We can only try to make up in activity what these competing nations accomplish through associating public and private interests in strengthening their economic positions."[36]

The policy of government aid certainly rested on wide agreement on the importance of exports, but its implementation fell somewhere beyond halfheartedness and considerably short of boldness. Wide agreement did not produce aggressiveness because the very economic interests that might be expected to spur government action were now concerned with other matters: expanding the tremendous home market and gaining tariff protection. In 1909, John Barrett, Director of the Bureau of American Republics, in an address before the National Association of Manufacturers, bemoaned the fact that in all the speeches in Congress over the new tariff bill, and in almost all the discussions in the newspapers, "there has been an absolute neglect of the effect the tariff may have on our export trade."[37] In brief, in spite of a consensus of opinion on the importance of foreign trade, government action was moderated by concerns that evoked a much greater response.

Having examined the two questions of the strengths and weaknesses of the China market at the turn of the century, and the degree of support provided by the Government in Washington in efforts to capture this market, the next question is whether the American business community demonstrated energy and imagination. Some of the Consuls stationed in major ports took a deep interest in the business activities of their fellow nationals and they prepared lengthy reports and wrote frequent letters containing detailed observations on commerce, the opportunities at hand, the factors making for success and failure, and the nature of the competition. In the 1890's, a majority of them filed optimistic reports and heralded even minor advances in sales of American goods, but throughout the hundreds of these reports and letters there is a common complaint of the lack of assertiveness on the part of American business concerns.

The apathy of American business concerns showed itself in a variety of ways. Consul John Fowler, stationed in the port of Chefoo, complained of the failure of American concerns to provide credit facilities, of the failure to send representatives to promote sales, and of the poor packaging of American goods.[38] These practices did not change. Eleven years later, in 1911, Consul George Anderson, in charge of the Consulate in Hongkong, attributed the decline in sales in recent years to the high prices of American goods, Japanese competition, failure to supply credit, poor packaging, and the lack of an effective sales organization.[39] Another official cited the failure of Americans to invest in China and reminded his readers that trade follows investment.[40] Vice-Consul-General Willard B. Hull, in Hankow, warned that American firms could not follow their present policies and hope to secure the business. "Nearly every American company represented in Hankow," wrote Hull, "has some European firm for its agent, and, naturally, American products will be sold only when these firms cannot secure the same things from their own country in Europe, thus keeping American goods, in most cases, as a second choice." Hull likewise advised that American manufacturers "must also count on giving longer credits if they wish to do business in this field."[41] Vice-Consul-General Percival Heintzleman in Shanghai, in 1908, stated that the three greatest handicaps of U.S. trade were: (1) failure to extend credit; (2) failure to send representatives; and (3) failure to invest American capital.[42] The Vice-Consul in Dalny, in 1909, deplored the failure to send representatives. American business, he observed, is in the hands of persons who are regarded as commercial rivals.[43]

American business, with the notable exception of Standard Oil, made no great effort to do what was necessary to sell to China. One major reason seems to have been the greener pastures near at hand. Consul George Anderson reported:

> They state frankly here that the cotton-goods market in the United States is so great, its demands so steady, the prices it pays so good, and its consumption so broad, that American manufacturers will give no more than passing interest to any foreign market and will not make the effort necessary to secure foreign business until home conditions turn against them.[44]

These observations lead to the conclusion that American business was apathetic or at least unimaginative in its methods.

United States Ministers in Peking often expressed regret over the lack of enterprise. In October, 1897, Charles Denby observed: "Unfortunately, our fellow-citizens have made no serious effort to avail themselves of the good will of China." Two years before a loan of one hundred million dollars had been offered to Americans, but he recorded: "I could find nobody in the United States that would touch it." American banking representatives had come to China but they were without authority to make a contract. Denby advised: "To accomplish anything here we must imitate the European powers and have fully authorized agents on the ground."[45]

Denby's successor, E. H. Conger, reported that Europeans were active in studying opportunities for railroads and mines. "If our capitalists," wrote Conger, "really desire a share they must have brains and money here."[46]

The apathy of American business in the China market did not correspond to their behavior elsewhere if we may assume that success in sales was a result of their initiative. Exports of manufactured goods increased dramatically. In 1890, they constituted only 12.48 percent of total exports; in 1900, they represented 31.65 percent of the total.[47] In 1910, the value reached $767 million compared to $122 million in 1880.[48]

An examination of figures on the China trade shows that it was limited to a very few commodities. Illuminating oil and cotton goods led the way by a wide margin. Tobacco and tobacco products ranked third and lumber was fourth. Analyzing these further, we find that unbleached cloth constituted the bulk of textiles. In the peak year, 1909, unbleached cloth exports totaled $6,983,774; bleached cloth was valued at $908,681 and colored cloth at $111,402.[49] The total exports of these three varieties in 1910 were $10,098,985 of unbleached, $1,351,040 of bleached and $8,521,466 of colored; of the total, China took $5,762,318 or approximately twenty-seven percent.[50] However, cotton textiles ranked eleventh among the exports of the United States in 1910 and accounted for only 1.95 percent of the value of all exports.[51]

Sales of illuminating oil totaled $1,251,201 in 1900, reached a peak for this period of $8,499,279 in 1908, and declined again to $5,016,397 in 1910. In the latter year, total exports of illuminating oil were valued at $62,477,527 and the Chinese market accounted for eight percent.[52]

The next most important item in the trade fell far below cotton cloth and oil. Exports to China of leaf tobacco amounted to $639,369 in 1906; dipped to $273,687 in 1909; and advanced to a peak of $653,496 in 1910.[53] Exports of cigarettes reached a high of $1,393,051 in 1907 and then slipped to $793,381 in 1908.[54] The chief lumber products exported to China were boards, deals and planes. These totaled $976,629 in 1907 but declined by fifty percent in 1909 and then recovered in part, amounting to $748,026 or two percent of total exports of these lumber items in 1910.[55]

These major exports represent the great bulk of the trade, $13,003,470 of a total of $16,181,670 in 1910. Sales of other important items were either trivial or nonexistent. Railway cars, carriages and other equipment varied; totaling only $382 in 1906, mounting to $137,439 in 1909 and then falling to $17,204 in 1910.[56] Sales of railway equipment to Japan in her sphere in China were greater. The rebuilding of the South Manchuria Railway, destroyed by the Russians during the war, was done largely with American-made equipment and in 1908 the sales totaled almost two million dollars. Rails, considered a separate item, were sold to Japan for use in China to the extent of $1,121,199.[57] But in the case of both equipment and rails, sales were trivial in most years. Locomotives, also considered a separate item, likewise were sold in large numbers ($2,404,619 worth in 1910) in one year and scarcely any in most years.[58]

The point that the sales of most manufactured items were small is well illustrated by the statistics for 1900. In that year,

American manufacturers sold $292 worth of cash registers, $6,345 of electrical supplies, $2,102 of laundry machinery, $17,520 of pumps and pumping machinery, and $7,769 of sewing machines. These were not the only items sold but they are representative. Obviously, these sales were scarcely adequate to excite the interest of the industrialists.

Contemporary observers of the China trade saw that the availability of credit and investment of American dollars were necessary for increasing sales. Recognition of this interdependence of trade and investment eventually encouraged bankers to show an interest in China but they found domestic American opportunities—and a few selective foreign ones—more promising. That the United States remained a debtor nation until World War I was, of course, of primary importance in explaining the absence of American capital in China.

Yet a transition was under way. Reviewing financial developments during the year 1900, the editor of the *Commercial and Financial Chronicle* noted that American bankers had been able to relieve Europe's loan requirements on several occasions. It was, he said, the first time that European Governments had turned to the United States for such help. The editor described this new development as marking "an epoch in American history." After 1900, investments abroad showed significant gains.

This change did not direct itself toward China except in a minor way. In his study of foreign investments in that country, C. F. Remer estimated the value of American business holdings in Shanghai in 1900 at ten million dollars and the value of their holdings throughout China at seventeen and one-half million dollars. Remer found that by 1915 the value of American investment in China was about forty-two million dollars. British, Japanese, Russian and French investment far surpassed that of America.

In the spring of 1909, the Department of State demanded that American bankers be granted entry into the Chinese loan market. This move grew out of the realization after the Russo-Japanese War that the commercial interests and political influence of the United States were on the decline. Equality of commercial opportunity had no real meaning when the nations that gained contracts for the railroads dictated the purchase of goods. This simple hypothesis, explaining the failure of the Americans to capture the China market, satisfied Philander Knox, the new Secretary of State under William Howard Taft. It likewise provided a rationale for Willard Straight who, as a Consul in Manchuria, had witnessed Japan's taking advantage of her military control to promote sales of Japanese goods. It was Straight, head of the newly created Division of Far Eastern Affairs, who pushed the Taft Administration into demanding that a consortium of American bankers be admitted to participation in the loans for financing the proposed construction of a railway network in central China. The European Governments and bankers gave reluctant consent to American participation but a prolonged hassle over the percentage of the total loans to be granted the Americans resulted in a long delay. It was the Department of State and not the bankers who insisted on an equal share for American capital.

In September of 1909, came the Knox proposal for an international loan to China enabling her to buy the railways in Manchuria owned by Japan and Russia. When this plan collapsed, the United States proposed a currency loan that would enable China to develop Manchuria. Again, Japan and Russia opposed the project and insisted on reservations to protect their own interests. The chief importance of both the railway project and the currency proposal lay in the fact that, for the first time, the U.S. Government sought to promote exports to China by means of American investment.

Measured against these actualities, the rhetoric concerning the China market was so wild as to suggest that it was in the nature of a myth. Indeed, the gap between the rhetoric and the actualities attained dimensions of such scope that one may assume that the sheer joy of the discussion and not facts sufficed as a propellant.

NOTES

1. Report of Rounseville Wildman, Consul-General in Hongkong, *Commercial Relations of the United States with Foreign Countries During the Year 1899* (Washington: U.S. Government Printing Office, 1900), I, 874.
2. Burlingame Johnson, Consul in Amoy, to Assistant Secretary of State David J. Hill, March 20, 1901. Hereafter consular dispatches cited are from the Department of State Archives. The author used the microfilm copies of these dispatches available in the Library at Michigan State University.
3. U.S., Bureau of Statistics, Department of State, *Special Consular Reports* (Reports from the Consuls of the United States in answer to circulars from the Department of State), *Highways of Commerce* (Washington: U.S. Government Printing Office, 1895), XII, 597.
4. *Ibid.*, 600.
5. James L. Rodgers, Consul in Shanghai, to the Department of State, January 8, 1906.
6. *Ibid.*
7. *Ibid.*
8. U.S., Bureau of Foreign Commerce, Department of State, *Special Consular Reports* (Washington: U.S. Government Printing Office, 1898), XVI, Part 1, 35.
9. The report published by the Imperial Maritime Customs Service entitled *An Inquiry into the Commercial Liabilities and Assets of China in International Trade* was forwarded by the U.S. Consul in Shanghai and is to be found in the dispatches from that Consulate.
10. Ralph W. Hidy and Muriel E. Hidy, *Pioneering in Big Business* (New York: Harper and Brothers, 1955), p. 152.
11. *Ibid.*, pp. 132–133, 259.
12. *Ibid.*, p. 267.
13. Samuel F. Gracey, Consul in Foochow, to Assistant Secretary of State Robert Bacon, December 6, 1906.
14. *Ibid.*
15. William Martin, Consul in Hankow, to Assistant Secretary of State Robert Bacon, February 6, 1906.
16. *Ibid.*, June 30, 1906.

17. Samuel Gracey, Consul in Foochow, to Assistant Secretary of State Robert Bacon, December 11, 1906.

18. *Ibid.*

19. E. H. Conger, Minister to China, to Secretary of State John Hay, November 3, 1898, Department of State Archives, microfilm copy in the Michigan State University Library. All copies of dispatches and instructions from and to the Minister in Peking cited hereafter used by the author were microfilm copies.

20. *Ibid.*

21. Charles Denby, Minister to China, to Secretary of State John Sherman, April 15, 1898.

22. E. H. Conger to Secretary of State William R. Day, July 31, 1898.

23. *Ibid.*, August 26, 1898.

24. An account of this episode is given in the author's *Open Door Diplomat: The Life of W. W. Rockhill* (Urbana: University of Illinois Press, 1952), pp. 72–76.

25. James Rodgers, Consul-General in Shanghai, to Assistant Secretary of State Francis B. Loomis, September 14, 1905.

26. Edward Bedloe, Consul in Canton, to Assistant Secretary of State William R. Day, April 7, 1898.

27. Edward Bedloe, Consul in Canton, to Assistant Secretary of State William R. Day, February 10, 1898. *See also* Bedloe's letters of April 11, 1898 and July 18, 1898.

28. Burlingame Johnson, Consul in Amoy, to the Department of State, June 26, 1897.

29. *Ibid.*, August 4, 1897.

30. William Martin, Consul in Hankow, to the Department of State, April 5, 1906.

31. *Ibid.*

32. John Fowler, Consul in Chefoo, to Secretary of State John Hay, May 29, 1905.

33. John Fowler, Consul in Chefoo, to Assistant Secretary of State Francis B. Loomis, August 11, 1905.

34. U.S., *Congressional Record*, 59th Congress, 1st Session, 1906, XL, Part 4, 3975.

35. C. S. Donaldson, "Government Assistance to Export Trade," *The Annals of the American Academy of Political and Social Science*, XXXIV (November, 1909), 555.

36. *Ibid.*

37. John Barrett, "South America—Our Manufacturers Greatest Opportunity," *The Annals of the American Academy of Political and Social Science*, XXXIV (November, 1909), 521.

38. John Fowler, "United States Trade at Chefoo," *Consular Reports Commerce, Manufactures, Etc.*, Nos. 220, 221, 222 and 223 (Washington: U.S. Government Printing Office, 1899), LIX (April, 1899), 550–551.

39. George Anderson, *Cotton-Goods Trade in China*, U.S. Department of

Commerce and Labor, *Special Consular Reports* No. 44 (Washington: U.S. Government Printing Office, 1911), pp. 14, 16, 17, 30.

40. *Commercial Relations of the United States with Foreign Countries During the Year 1907*, I (Washington: U.S. Government Printing Office, 1908), *see* Consul-General Charles Denby, "Review of Trade Conditions of China," 345.

41. *Ibid., see* report of Willard B. Hull, Vice-Consul in Hankow, "Hankow," 378.

42. Percival Heintzleman, "China, Review of Trade Conditions," *Commercial Relations of the United States with Foreign Countries During the Year 1908* (Washington: U.S. Government Printing Office, 1909), II, 413–414.

43. Report of Adolph A. Williamson, Vice-Consul in Dalny, *Commercial Relations of the United States with Foreign Countries During the Year 1909* (Washington: U.S. Government Printing Office, 1910), p. 739. Williamson wrote: "This decline of American trade is in part due to the absence of American effort, coupled with the energy of English and Japanese competitors, the Germans showing more interest toward the close of the year. There are no American houses established here and the agencies are in the hands of persons who are regarded as commercial rivals. Under such conditions not much increase of American trade is to be expected."

44. George Anderson, *Cotton-Goods Trade in China*, U.S. Department of Commerce and Labor, *Special Consular Reports* No. 44 (Washington: U.S. Government Printing Office, 1911), p. 30.

45. Charles Denby to Secretary of State John Sherman, October 20, 1897.

46. E. H. Conger to Secretary of State William R. Day, July 31, 1898.

47. U.S., Bureau of the Census, *Statistical Abstract of the United States: 1901* (Washington: U.S. Government Printing Office, 1901), p. 187.

48. U.S., Department of Commerce and Labor, *The Foreign Commerce and Navigation of the United States for the Year Ending June 30, 1910* (Washington: U.S. Government Printing Office, 1910), p. 19.

49. *Ibid.,* pp. 544–548.

50. *Ibid.*

51. *Ibid.,* p. 58.

52. *Ibid.,* p. 692.

53. *Ibid.,* p. 738.

54. *Ibid.,* p. 740.

55. *Ibid.,* p. 756.

56. *Ibid.,* p. 518.

57. *Ibid.,* p. 608.

58. *Ibid.,* p. 627.
For more specific facts concerning Japan's purchase of railway equipment in the United States for the rebuilding of the South Manchuria Railway, *see* report of Roger S. Greene, Consul in Dalny, *Commercial*

Relations of the United States with Foreign Countries During the Year 1907 (Washington: U.S. Government Printing Office, 1908), I, 360.

The facts on the American China Development Company are derived from the material in the Department of State Archives. For a full account of the diplomatic aspects, *see* William Braisted, "The United States and the American China Development Company," *The Far Eastern Quarterly*, XI (February, 1952), 147–165.

CHAPTER IV

MANCHURIA AND RUSSO-AMERICAN RIVALRY

THE HOPE for a market for American goods in China was no less of a driving force because it was illusory, and the myth played a prominent role in American concern over the threatened dominance of Russia over Manchuria. North China and Manchuria served as the market for approximately ninety percent of the cotton goods entering China from the United States. The value of American goods entering Newchwang, the major port in Manchuria, in 1898 was $11,911,339.[1] Consequently, Russian moves in 1898 and after aroused apprehension. In April, 1899, John Fowler, viewing the scene from the Consulate in Chefoo, warned:

> We thus see that our best market, not only for oil, but for all our products, is in imminent danger; for no one believes that the Russians will not soon control the markets for the sale of their products—oil, cottons, etc.,—in all the territory north of this. . . .[2]

Six months after Fowler made this observation, Hay's dispatch of the Open Door Notes provided a test of Russian intentions. In St. Petersburg, Ambassador Charlemagne Tower conferred with Count Muraviev, the Russian Minister for Foreign Affairs. Muraviev questioned Tower closely as to the precise meaning of the Notes. While willing to commit his Government to the principle of equality of commercial opportunity within a sphere of influence, he remained unwilling to widen this principle to the leased territory. He also objected to committing his Government to equal railway rates for Russian nationals and others. Muraviev, as a matter of fact, objected to any form of a written agreement that might, sometime in the future, haunt his countrymen in some way not foreseeable at the moment.

In Washington, Rockhill met with the same reservations as he sought to negotiate with Count Cassini, the Russian Ambassador. The final outcome of this sparring was that Russia consented to Hay's announcing that she agreed to the principle of equality of commercial opportunity, an innocuous gesture that left her free of specific commitments.[3]

Developments in Manchuria following the Boxer uprising aroused further alarm, and Russia became the chief diplomatic antagonist. Manchuria, in 1900, was a vast undeveloped territory. Its importance rested in its potential, not in its economic status. Russia and Japan were also concerned about its importance to their future security. Insofar as Americans looked upon Manchuria as a strategic problem, they feared that if Russia controlled Manchuria, she would dominate the Peking Government.

In the late autumn of 1901, Captain James H. Reeves, the U.S. military attaché in Peking, made an extensive trip through Manchuria.[4] Everywhere he received the cooperation of the Russians who were energetically at work on the construction of the Chinese Eastern Railway and in the building of facilities in the new railway towns of Dalny, Mukden and Harbin. At Dalny new docks were under construction, streets were laid out for prospective inhabitants, and the harbor was being improved. Similar projects were under way at Harbin and Mukden. At Newchwang the railroad facilities were being enlarged. Only at Port Arthur had there been little or no improvement since the Russian occupation.

Mukden, the largest city, had a population estimated at two hundred thousand; Kirin, located in Mongolia but also under Russian control, was approximately the same size: Newchwang had some thirty-six thousand inhabitants; Harbin consisted of a series of old villages and was little more than a camp for railway workers; Tieh-ling, the most important market on the Liao River north of Newchwang had some forty thousand inhabitants; and Dalny's population consisted wholly of Russian railway workers, Chinese coolies employed in building the city, and a few merchants. Most of Manchuria, and especially the northern half, was only sparsely settled.

This vast frontier had all the markings of a newly opened

territory. Robber bands roamed at will not far from Kirin and especially on the border of Korea. The Chinese Eastern Railway was, in large part, ill built. The tracks in some places rested on nothing more than tree branches, and the passenger cars were unbelievably filthy. In the cities there was no provision for either water or sewage. The railway workers and the railway guards were a rough and poorly disciplined lot.

This area, resembling in many ways the Rocky Mountain territories in the post Civil War era, became the focal point of international diplomacy immediately after the Boxer Revolt. Russia was already well on the way to making Manchuria her own preserve prior to the Boxer uprising. She had gained China's assent to building the Chinese Eastern Railway. The proposed line enabled her to take a shortcut from her Trans-Siberian line across northern Manchuria to Vladivostok. She also acquired the right to build a line from Harbin, on the former route, southward to Port Arthur, thereby giving her access to southern Manchuria and the northern provinces of China Proper. To carry on this construction program, Russia established the Russo-Chinese Bank. To protect her enterprises, she exercised the right acquired by treaty to station railway guards in the towns along the railway and to patrol the lines.

When the Boxers, joined by regular Chinese troops, swarmed over the Russian enterprises in the summer of 1900, driving Russian settlers before them and destroying railway lines and equipment, Russia responded vigorously. She dispatched to the area approximately eight times as many troops as comprised the international expedition sent to rescue the besieged Legations in Peking. At the close of hostilities she made it clear that she would not let this occasion pass without achieving security for her Manchurian interests. This, as Russia saw it, was a matter to be settled between herself and China. Her unilateral action set off a flood of accusations to the effect that she aimed at complete domination of Manchuria and the probable extinction of Chinese sovereignty in the area.

Captain Reeves gave his estimates of the situation. What were Russia's future intentions? Reeves concluded that the military situation did not give much evidence as to what these were. He noted: "The number of troops in Manchuria is not so great as is usually reported, nor do I believe they are as formidable as generally reported to be." He estimated the number, if railway guards were included, to be about thirty-five thousand. The railway guards, while of a military nature, were under the Ministry for Finance. The guards were stationed along the railway, and patrols were sent out before the passage of each train. Reeves thought the military force more than adequate to hold the country but he also observed that the deep hostility of the Chinese in Manchuria toward the Russians and the success of the Chinese during the Boxer troubles in destroying the railway should not be discounted. The Chinese, he thought, would welcome an opportunity "to try it again."

A weakness in Russia's position lay in the rivalry of the military and civilian organizations. "The military people regard with disdain and scorn all civil officials, and the latter return the feeling with interest . . . but in spite of all this and all other imperfections and drawbacks," Reeves concluded, "the grand opportunity seems to have arrived for Russia's expansion in the East and she knows it and is going to take advantage of it. . . . While other nations may object and protest against Russia's course, I doubt if there is one that would not do the same if in Russia's position."

Would Russia permit other nations commercial entry? Reeves did not know. American goods were more prominent in the shops of Manchurian towns than the goods of any other nation. Two American firms, Clarkson and Company and the American Trading Company, operated in Manchuria but the former was more active in Siberia than in Manchuria. Reeves considered the policy of the American Trading Company shortsighted for "the company does for the most part its exploitation by means of catalogues and price lists and a few samples." It was the general opinion of those with whom he had met that "what is most needed is a warehouse at two or three of the larger centers and a fair supply of goods always kept on hand." He had also heard "the usual complaint . . . that the American goods are not properly packed." American manufacturing interests ought to send a well-informed man to Manchuria to learn what was necessary. "Of course," wrote Reeves, "if Russia is not going to allow a business man in the country unless he be a Russian subject, then the questions presented are more difficult." "But," he observed, "Russia has not committed herself to any such policy and there may be ways to avoid such action on her part."

Reeves viewed the whole situation with philosophical tranquility and many Americans shared his attitude. Regarding the future of this tremendous area and the presence of the Russians, Senator John T. Morgan of Alabama, long known for his support of expansionism, broke with his past record and argued that the United States should assist Russia in taking over Manchuria. This would promote peace and order and the development of a market for American cotton goods. It would do even more, said the Senator; Russian gratitude would lead to a long-term friendship between the two nations.[5] Perhaps if the interest in markets had been purely economic, Morgan's views would have prevailed.

Other important and well-organized American interests did not view the situation with aloofness. They saw Russia's actions as injurious to the economic well-being of the United States and, more important, as a threat to the security of the nation as a Pacific Power.

The American Asiatic Association spoke for those who shared these fears. Its membership included the highly successful importers and exporters and the leading textile manufacturers. John Foord, Executive Secretary of the Association and confidant of Presidents and Secretaries of State, was constantly called upon to advise the Department of State. For instance, after the Boxer Revolt when preparations began for the negotiation of a new commercial treaty with China, Foord and a delegation of leaders of the Association were invited to Washington by President McKinley for consultation. The draft of the proposed treaty was in very large part prepared by Foord.[6] The Association's annual dinners in New York provided the public with a view of the cordial relations that existed between it and the officials of the Department of State and members of Congress who always attended.[7]

The community of interests represented by the American Asiatic Association had the *Journal of Commerce and Commercial Bulletin* as its most able and thoughtful public spokesman. This New York weekly newspaper provided its readers with detailed reports on all aspects of American business. Editorially, it championed the expansion of commerce by means of a reciprocal trade program. Probably no journal gave so much attention to the rising ascendancy of American industry and the need for foreign markets, and its highly knowledgeable writers spoke to and for the business community in measured words and with carefully reasoned arguments.

The editors viewed China as of major importance to the future of the United States. In the years after the Boxer Revolt their attention focused on Manchuria and the Russian problem, and with this as the focus they developed a view that comprehended not only questions of commerce but the issue of Chinese exclusion and the broader question of Russian domination of all of East Asia. In arguing that the United States could not avoid a stark confrontation with Russia, the editors took satisfaction in having "got to the heart of the matter." Their view is important to understanding the policy that was in the process of emerging in Washington. However, the complexities of the political arena and a different estimate of the importance of Manchuria inhibited those charged with foreign affairs from acting boldly.

The major antagonists, as the New York editors saw the world, were the United States and Russia. Since 1895, the latter country had moved down from the Amur River and over Chinese territory with one ultimate goal in mind, control of Manchuria. The Boxer Revolt furnished Russia with pretexts for new advances in that direction. While others sought compensation for injuries in the form of indemnity payments or commercial concessions, the Russian Government "executed a clever flank movement" offering to accept territorial compensation in Manchuria.[8]

The editors never tired of citing the importance of American trade at Newchwang, at the mouth of the Liao River, the major port of entry for Manchuria. This trade would be eliminated by the Russians. Thirty-one percent of the foreign trade of that port was in American goods and its value amounted to 6,474,895 haikwan taels in 1899.[9]

Not unmindful of the fact that these statistics provided less than a thumping affirmation of the importance of Manchuria as a market, the editors bolstered their case with the assertion that even the loss of a small sector of an industry's total market could be most damaging.

The Boxer disturbances, by shutting off that market, had led to the demoralization of the entire textile industry, in both the north and south. In an editorial entitled "Value of the Open Door" the writer said cotton textile exports to China totaled only $9,823,253 in the fiscal year 1899 and $8,783,134 in 1900.[10] That an industry whose total annual output was valued at $339,198,619 should have been so seriously affected provided an "impressive illustration of the value of an export outlet for the surplus products of our manufactures. . . ." At the annual dinner of the American Asiatic Association in May, 1902, Senator McLaurin of South Carolina spoke even more strongly of the importance of the China market. "In 1890 we had thirty-four cotton mills in South Carolina; in 1900 we had eighty. . . . The product increased in value from $10,000,000 to $30,000,000 and almost all, or at least the bulk of the products of these mills goes directly to China." [11]

Having demonstrated that the Manchurian market was vital to the welfare of the American textile industry, it was no less important to show that Russia would exclude American trade. Speculating on the significance of each Russian action or lack of action, the editors soon constructed a case against any possibility of Russia honoring the virtuous American principle of equality of commercial opportunity. Developments at Newchwang under Russian occupation looked like bold discrimination against all foreign trade. Russia collected the customs in Newchwang and favored her own imports. She fostered the growth of Dalny, a terminal point on her railway, where she could exercise permanent control with the aim of undermining the position of Newchwang.[12] When the editors learned that the telegraph lines out of Newchwang had yet to be restored, they saw this as a device for cutting off foreign trade.

They maintained that it was foolish to believe that Russia would countenance equal commercial opportunity for other nations. Russia's economic policy was to discourage foreign trade. The exports of the United States to Russia totaled less than those to Denmark by four million dollars and also less than exports to Sweden.[13] The Government of Russia was a partner of private business and aimed at developing industry and making the country self-sufficient. The editors noted that Vladivostok, formerly a free port, had its status changed in 1901. They cited the testimony of Russian leaders who said Russia could not compete in the Chinese market and therefore felt compelled "to erect artificial barriers against all commerce except her own."

In an editorial entitled "Mischief in Manchuria" the writer portrayed what he considered the realities. "The Siberian and Eastern Chinese lines, are intended to foster Russian trade with China, and to oust foreign competitors there. . . . That is what the Russian Government says when addressing Russians; it is what they have led Muscovite merchants to believe, and it is what Americans and Europeans trading with Chinese ports know to be the case." He cited Mr. Merkuloff of the Society for the Promotion of Russian Trade and Industry who had said the railway was an inadequate protector of Russian commercial interests and that new means must be devised "for preventing the entry of foreign merchandise into Manchuria." [14]

Conscious that the immigration question stood as a major obstacle to good relations with China, the editors of the *Journal of Commerce* kept a close watch on government policy on this issue. In 1902, Congress was engaged in a debate over Chinese exclusion and a bill before the Senate called for an even stricter policy than the existing Geary Act. John Foord and other members of the American Asiatic Association appeared before Congressional committees to protest that the exclusion policy would lead the Chinese to retaliate and curtail the sale of American goods.[15]

The *Journal of Commerce* campaigned vigorously against the exclusion of Chinese. It cited, with approval, the testimony of Silas D. Webb, President of the China and Japan Trading Company. Webb declared that the "insulting and humiliating restrictions which the Chinese Exclusion Act had placed on the entry of Chinese merchants, travelers and students into this country seemed likely to undo all the advantage we had gained through the friendly attitude of our Government during the recent negotiations between the Powers and China." [16]

The newspaper's forthright position went beyond those who called for fair treatment but favored exclusion of Chinese laborers. "There is no argument that can be urged against keeping out the Canton coolie, who is the only type of Chinese laborer

we know," wrote the editor, "which would not equally apply to
the exclusion of the lowest class of Poles, Hungarians, and Ital-
ians who come here without any question being raised in regard
to their race or nationality." To the alarmists who feared inundation if any relaxation of the policy took place, he said:
"There is not the slightest danger of the country being overrun
by any such Mongolian horde as the anti-Chinese agitators have
depicted as ready for the invasion of these shores."[17]

Early in 1902, the editor reprimanded Theodore Roosevelt
for supporting Chinese exclusion.[18] While the *Journal* decried
the fact that Southern Senators and Congressmen supported exclusion legislation, it noted with approval the testimony of A. J.
Milstead, who was financially interested in a number of southern
cotton mills, when he said: "We need China as a market, and it
certainly is not common sense to suppose we can insult our
customers and at the same time expect preferential treatment
from them." [19]

On the question of the trade policy in the Philippines, the
editors again made their guide the importance of the China
market. The United States, they argued, must pursue the policy
of the Open Door if it was to promote this policy in China.[20]

When discussing the larger question of what Far Eastern
policy ought to be, the writers for the *Journal of Commerce*
hinged their whole case on the commercial issue. The Department of State, they wrote, "shows more and more convincingly
as successive occasions arise, that the conduct of our foreign
affairs is governed by the principle that the most important of
all our international relations consists in keeping the outlets we
have secured by treaty and finding new ones for the surplus
products of American industry." [21]

Regarding the Russian policy in Manchuria the editors repeatedly called for the United States to take a decided stand.
They would have preferred calling Russia's procedure "an un-
friendly act," a strong term in diplomacy. In March, 1901, the
editor, impatient with the caution shown by Secretary of State
John Hay, said that the United States was "in a position to lend
a powerful impulse to greater unity of action (among the
powers), and it is to be hoped that no weak fear of foreign
entanglements will operate to allow the opportunity to slip." [22]

Those who lamented that the United States had become a world power were out of touch. Was the United States to make polite remonstrations when other nations unjustly discriminate against American commerce? [23]

Although equality of commercial opportunity was the goal emphasized, it was tied to China's territorial and administrative integrity. In March, 1901, aroused by reports of Russian pressure on China, the American Asiatic Association resolved that the United States must protest because if Russia's proposal were not challenged, "it must inevitably become permanent and thus lead to the territorial dismemberment of the Chinese Empire, and no further step of that process could be consistently opposed if consent be, openly or tacitly, given to this one." [24]

The passing of time, to say nothing of much rhetoric, assured the easy passage of this opinion into the realm of conviction. The process did not stop there but rather continued until, by the summer of 1903, the threads of antagonism had woven themselves into a world view.

In yet another editorial in the *Journal of Commerce*, entitled "American Interests in the Pacific," the controversy took on the dimensions of a full-scale confrontation between Russia and the United States. The question of equality of commercial opportunity was insignificant in the broader picture of Russia's occupation of Manchuria. "The whole question of the integrity of the Chinese Empire, and consequently of Russia's predominance in Eastern Asia, turns upon the recognition or denial of Chinese sovereignty in the territory now occupied by Russian troops." If Russia achieved dominance in Mukden, she would soon do the same in Peking and then Germany would take Shantung and France would take Yunnan. "It is not alone that the commerce of the United States has much to lose and nothing to gain by the division of the Chinese Empire, that it becomes the duty of our Government to watch and protest against the first insidious advances toward such a consummation." The major and all-important reason for a strong stand was that if Russia were permitted to continue "it is only a question of time when Russia would become the dominant power in Asia and on the western shore of the Pacific Ocean." The editor termed the prospect "a serious menace to the material and political development of the

United States." "That is to say," he explained, "the course of natural evolution which would make this country the dominant power of the Pacific would be effectually arrested, to the manifest detriment of every industrial and commercial interest in this republic." [25]

But in 1903, other considerations arrested the drive of those in political authority from a precipitous decision. Even in the American Asiatic Association some leaders showed restraint. James S. Fearon, a senior member of a firm in the China trade and an agent of the International Banking Corporation, did not object to Russia controlling northern Manchuria. He was also uncertain as to the degree of Russian determination. In a speech Fearon explained: "A few strong men lead her that way. There are other strong men who desire time for the consolidation of what she already has. Her councils are far from being undivided, and the ambitions of the adventurous ones, while acquiesced in so long as they cause no danger to the State, would be repudiated rather than seriously risk war." [26]

The editor of the *New York Daily Tribune* censured Russia and sympathized with China but then concluded that "it would be difficult to define adequate grounds for giving her any more than sympathy." "The promise of evacuation," he wrote, "was made by Russia to China." China alone could call upon Russia to redeem the promise. American interest in Manchuria was commercial, not political. It made no difference to the United States who governed Manchuria.[27]

The Americans in general showed no interest in the Manchurian question. Other issues of a domestic nature now occupied them. President Theodore Roosevelt was inclined to see the struggle among the world powers in bold and sweeping generalizations, but he was also an astute politician, sensitive to popular prejudices and long habits of thought. In May, 1903, he wrote to John Hay:

> As for China, I do not see that there is anything we can say, even by way of suggestion. The mendacity of the Russians is something appalling. The bad feature of the situation from our standpoint is that as yet it seems that we cannot fight to keep Manchuria open.[28]

Roosevelt limited himself to protests in behalf of the equality of commercial opportunity. Yet he also felt the tug of the same arguments set forth by the editors of the *Journal of Commerce*. In July, 1903, he confided to Hay:

> I have not the slightest objection to the Russians knowing that I feel thoroughly aroused and irritated at their conduct in Manchuria, but I don't intend to give way and that I am year-by-year growing more confident that this country would back me in going to an extreme in the matter.[29]

Another development in the summer of 1903 may have contributed to the general ambivalence on the China question although there is no evidence of its having any influence. Unsold stocks of American cotton goods piled up in Shanghai, reportedly because of a financial crisis in Tientsin. Merchants talked of reexporting some of the goods back to the United States, and there was a general lack of confidence.[30]

The response of the Department of State to the Manchurian question reflected, in part, the point of view of the *Journal of Commerce*. Nevertheless, official policy differed very significantly from the program advocated by that journal.

NOTES

1. John Fowler, "United States Trade in China," *Consular Reports Commerce, Manufactures, Etc.* (Washington: U.S. Government Printing Office, 1899), LXI (December, 1899), 79.
2. John Fowler, "United States Trade at Chefoo," *Consular Reports Commerce, Manufactures, Etc.*, Nos. 220, 221, 222 and 223 (Washington: U.S. Government Printing Office, 1899), LIX (April, 1899), 550.
3. Edward H. Zabriskie, *American–Russian Rivalry in the Far East: A Study in Diplomacy and Power Politics 1895–1914* (Philadelphia: University of Pennsylvania Press, 1946), pp. 55–59.
4. Captain James H. Reeves presented a fifty-two-page typewritten report to E. H. Conger, the U.S. Minister to China. Conger forwarded the report to Washington on February 6, 1902. The report is available in the file "Dispatches from United States Ministers to China" in the Department of State Archives.
5. Editor, "Value of the Open Door," *The Journal of Commerce and Commercial Bulletin,* April 11, 1902, p. 4.
6. John Foord, Secretary of the American Asiatic Association to President William McKinley, January 25, 1901, "Dispatches from United States Ministers to China," Department of State Archives.
7. *The Journal of Commerce and Commercial Bulletin* provided detailed stories, including a list of those present, of the annual dinners. For an example, *see* "Favorable Outlook for the Open Door to China," May 26, 1902, p. 8.
8. "Treating with China on Trade Privileges," *The Journal of Commerce and Commercial Bulletin,* January 21, 1901, p. 8.
9. Editor, "Halting Diplomacy," *ibid.,* March 25, 1901, p. 4.
10. Editor, "Value of the Open Door," *ibid.,* April 11, 1902, p. 4.
11. "Favorable Outlook for the Open Door in China," *ibid.,* May 26, 1902, p. 8.
12. Editor, "A Question of American Interest," *ibid.,* April 1, 1901, p. 4; editor, "The Anglo–Japanese Treaty," *ibid.,* February 17, 1902, p. 4.
13. Editor, "Our Export Trade with Russia," *ibid.,* February 18, 1901, p. 4.
14. "Mischief in Manchuria," *ibid.,* June 22, 1903, p. 7.
15. "Chinese Exclusion Injurious to Trade," *ibid.,* January 27, 1902.
16. "Inequitable Treatment of Chinese Merchants," *ibid.,* December 16, 1901, p. 8.

17. Editor, "The Chinese Exclusion Policy," *ibid.*, December 30, 1901, p. 4.
18. Editor, "Chinese Exclusion and Commercial Suicide," *ibid.*, January 13, 1902, p. 4.
19. "Cotton Goods Interests Ask Fair Play for China," *ibid.*, January 13, 1902.
20. Editor, "American Enterprise in the Far East," *ibid.*, January 20, 1902.
21. Editor, "Diplomacy as an Aid to Commerce," *ibid.*, March 3, 1902.
22. Editor, "The Negotiations at Pekin," *ibid.*, March 25, 1901, p. 4.
23. Editor, "Halting Diplomacy," *ibid.*, March 25, 1901, p. 4.
24. *Ibid.*
25. Editor, "American Interests in the Pacific," *ibid.*, July 13, 1903, p. 4.
26. "Situation in China of Commerce and Politics," *ibid.*, October 12, 1903, p. 8.
27. Editor, "Our Interest in Manchuria," *New York Daily Tribune*, November 8, 1903.
28. Elting E. Morison (ed.), *The Square Deal, 1901–1903*, Vol. III: *The Letters of Theodore Roosevelt* (Cambridge: Harvard University Press, 1951), p. 209.
29. *Ibid.*, p. 520.
30. "American Cotton Goods Depressed in China," *The Journal of Commerce and Commercial Bulletin*, July 6, 1903, p. 8.

CHAPTER V

THE DIPLOMATS AND RUSSIA

EVENTS moved with rapidity following the dispatch of the Open Door Notes in September, 1899. Public acclaim of the announced policy provided a strong impetus. Then the direct involvement of the United States in China during the Boxer catastrophe and in the Conference of Ministers in Peking built up the momentum toward full-scale involvement in East Asia. The activities of the American Asiatic Association and the editorial campaign of the *Journal of Commerce* in the years 1901 to 1904 helped provide public support for a firm policy.

Japan's decisiveness in opposing Russia in February, 1901, created an atmosphere which encouraged the Administration of Theodore Roosevelt to follow such a course. Earlier there had been some uneasiness about Japan. In the summer of 1899 she sought to gain a concession at Amoy in Fukien Province. Her demands upon the local Taotai called for setting aside a large part of the waterfront for the use of Japanese merchant ships, thereby endangering the access of the Americans to Amoy, the chief port for trade between China and the Philippines. The United States protested and succeeded in limiting the extent of the concession.[1]

In March, 1900, the Japanese were so militant that fear arose that they aimed at taking over Fukien.[2] In the fall of 1900, Rockhill, then in Peking, showed uneasiness concerning Japan's intentions. He wrote to Hay, saying he would not be surprised if Japan and Russia came to an agreement dividing Manchuria and Korea between themselves. Had Japan aligned herself with Russia, as Rockhill feared, then the United States would have found it futile to pursue a course in opposition to Russia.

However, with Japan's bold opposition in February, 1901,

Hay had reason to believe that he could safely protest against Russia's efforts to control Manchuria. Japan and Great Britain, owing to their entrenched interests, would be in the forefront and face the greatest risks. Therefore, the United States could, without danger, protest against aggressive moves by the Government in St. Petersburg.

When Count Witte informed Kuropatkin, Russia's Minister for War, of the Boxer uprising, Kuropatkin welcomed the report with the statement "this gives us a reason to take over Manchuria." [3] Witte, who preferred peaceful economic penetration, appealed to Li Hung-chang, the Emperor's representative, for the cooperation of Chinese troops in protecting the Chinese Eastern Railway. Li, on June 29, 1900, urged the Tartar Generals in Manchuria to protect the Russian line. The generals were unable to control their men and before long both Boxers and Chinese troops attacked Russian property and personnel. In response, Russia dispatched more than one hundred and seventy-three thousand troops to Manchuria. In a short time they occupied not only Manchuria but large parts of North China, including the important treaty port of Newchwang, and then seized the railways from Peking to Tientsin and Shanhaikwan. Although the military occupation was easily achieved, the Russians reported continued disturbances and consequent danger to property and nationals. Nor had the military moves come soon enough to prevent extensive damage to the Chinese Eastern Railway. The Russians saw the hostilities as constituting a war.[4] It was on the basis of this view that Russia felt wholly justified in separating what took place in Manchuria from the Allied Expedition to rescue the foreign Legations in Peking.

The other Powers, including the United States, did not see it in this light. The first intimation of Russian intentions to deal with China independently came on August 29, 1900, shortly after the lifting of the siege of the Legations, when the Russian Chargé d'Affaires notified the acting Secretary of State Alvey A. Adee that the Government of Russia had ordered the withdrawal of her Minister in Peking, his staff, and the troops who had participated in the Allied Expedition. The Department of State promptly affirmed that the interests of all would best be served by joint negotiations. "Any power which determines to withdraw its troops from Peking," wrote Adee, "will necessarily proceed thereafter to protect its interests in China by its own method, ..."[5]

Count Lamsdorf, Russia's Minister for Foreign Affairs, justified the separate course of action as necessary to facilitate the return of the Chinese Government to Peking where it could conduct negotiations free of the duress that a military occupation necessarily implied. Seeking to allay suspicion of Russian motives, Lamsdorf explained that the presence of Russian troops in Manchuria and other parts of North China, was a temporary measure. Russia, he said, had no intention whatever of seeking to acquire "a single inch of territory in either China or Manchuria."[6] Shortly afterward, Lamsdorf elaborated upon this explanation. He cited the continued disorders in Manchuria and pointed out how they endangered Russia's extensive interests. Also, he argued, the hostilities in Manchuria were different in nature and scope from the Allied Campaign in Peking.[7]

The United States, Great Britain and Japan rejected Lamsdorf's argument. They maintained that all the nations participating in the Peking Campaign should submit all questions arising out of the revolt to the Ministers acting jointly in Peking. The independent course of St. Petersburg aroused their suspicions and their skepticism rapidly increased as Russia shielded her negotiations with China under a cloak of secrecy.

The lifting of the siege in Peking and the defeat of the Chinese troops in Manchuria caused Tseng Ch'i, a Tartar General in Manchuria, to send a representative to the headquarters of the Russian commander, Admiral Alexieff, to arrange a truce. The agreement, drafted by the Russians, was signed by the Chinese representatives under duress. Exceeding military considerations of the moment, it provided for Chinese demobilization in Manchuria, temporary Russian occupation, and for the appointment of a Russian Political Resident stationed in Mukden "to whom the Tartar General must give all information respecting any important measures."[8] Li Hung-chang learned of the agreement but did not inform the Imperial Court until January 15. The Court immediately rejected it.

In the meantime, another set of demands had been drafted

in St. Petersburg. The new demands, incorporated in a memorandum entitled "The Establishment of Russian Supervision in Manchuria," were formulated by Count Witte and his two colleagues, the Minister for Foreign Affairs, Lamsdorf, and the Minister for War, Kuropatkin. A set of proposals, based on this draft, was handed to the Chinese Minister in St. Petersburg on February 16, 1901.

Because of the importance of these proposals and the necessity of distinguishing between them and the garbled versions that became public at the time, it is useful to cite the major points of the program presented by Lamsdorf. Russia agreed to the restoration of the Chinese Government in Manchuria. Russian troops would assist the railway guards in protecting the Chinese Eastern Railway. Chinese troops were to be withdrawn and permitted to return only after the completion of the railway and then only after the number of troops had been agreed upon with Russia. Outside the railway district, order was to be maintained by Chinese police guards, the number to be determined by agreement with the Russian Government. China was to bind herself not to grant any concessions for railroads, the working of mines or any industrial enterprises to foreign powers in Manchuria, Mongolia, Tarbagatai, Ili, Kashgar, Yorkand, Khotan, and Keri. In these territories China was not to build railroads nor grant parcels of land to foreigners, except in Newchwang, without the agreement of Russia. China was to promise to the Chinese Eastern Railway the right to build a railway to the Great Wall.[9]

Rumors of the Tseng-Alexieff Agreement, and then of the new negotiations, began to circulate among the representatives of the other Powers in January. The first responses showed a cautious mood in London and Washington, but Japan reacted sharply and asked the British to join her in protesting to Peking against any separate agreements. The British took time to explore German intentions. However, agreement was reached and in the middle of February, Japan, Great Britain, and Germany warned China of the dangers in accepting the reputed Russian proposals.[10]

The rumors of Russian negotiations led to American protests. At first, Secretary of State John Hay steered cautiously away from political questions. On February 1, he telegraphed the Powers concerned protesting the terms of the Tseng-Alexieff Agreement, but on the same day he also replied to an inquiry from Japan in a manner that is an excellent illustration of Hay's ambivalence on the China question.[11] The United States, he said, was "not at present prepared to attempt singly or in concert with other powers to uphold China's integrity by a demonstration which could present a character of hostility to any other power."[12] Yet, on February 19, Hay sent essentially the same protest to Peking as had been made by Japan, Great Britain, and Germany.[13]

While Japan's anxiety mounted and led to the consideration of war, provided an arrangement could be reached with Great Britain, Hay teetered between his loyalty to the principles of the Open Door and his reluctance to become deeply involved. In a conversation with Count Cassini, the Russian Ambassador in Washington, Hay, according to Cassini, stated:

> We fully recognize Russia's right to adopt such measures as she considers necessary to prevent the repetition of the grievous events of last year. We would even have understood if she had gone further along this path, insofar as it could be acknowledged necessary for her interests and projects, if we have the assurance that our trade would not suffer and that the door would remain open.[14]

Hay, at this early stage, limited himself to taking a stand on the principle of equality of commercial opportunity, the principle to which he was inextricably committed by his Notes of September, 1899.

In the meantime, Russia on the one hand and Japan and Great Britain on the other, mounted pressure in China in accordance with their respective interests. Russia held the advantage, being in possession of Manchuria. However, Russia did yield to Chinese requests for modification of many of the points included in the draft of February 16. The revised draft did not include the right to build a railroad to the Great Wall. China would be permitted to station troops in Manchuria, subject to prior consultation with Russia. The prohibition against Chinese arms was lifted and a new clause specified that the regulation of imports of arms and ammunition should be in accord with the general agreement to be concluded by the conference in Peking. Indemnities for damage done to the Chinese Eastern

Railway would also be determined "in accordance with the principles of assessment to be agreed upon between the foreign representatives at Peking and to be approved by the Powers." Russia's
earlier proposal that she should have exclusive rights to build
railways and develop mines in the vast areas bordering on her
frontier would be limited to Manchuria.[15] Both Li Hung-chang
and the Chinese Minister in St. Petersburg, Yang Ju, argued in
favor of acceptance on the grounds that refusal would result in
the loss of Manchuria.[16]

The Imperial Court found itself under pressure to reject the
Russian proposal. The three leading southern Viceroys strongly
opposed the agreement. Chang Chih-tung, probably the most influential of the Viceroys, maintained that the Russian concessions
related only to minor details. All three Viceroys placed their
hopes on encouraging the other Powers to intervene.[17] Their
efforts to dissuade the Court received the unequivocal support
of Japan and Great Britain and, to a lesser extent of the United
States. As a result, the Court stood firm. Confronted by opposition on all sides, Russia withdrew her demands early in April,
1901.

This withdrawal was dictated by considerations of expediency
rather than by a change in aims. New negotiations were soon in
progress and, in the meantime, Russia continued to hold the
advantages she had gained in Manchuria. None of her actions
was more disturbing to the United States than her complete
control of Newchwang, a treaty port which had served as a gateway for the entry of American goods. On August 29, 1901, Hay
cabled Conger:

> Confidential, Russian encroachments Newchwang causes anxiety.
> . . . Note especially any damage to American trade. Give opinions
> of your colleagues as far as attainable.[18]

But Hay was also concerned over the broader problem, and
rumors of the Russo-Chinese negotiations led him to urge Conger, on November 14, to watch these events and get what information he could from Japan's Minister in Peking.[19] Hay's
uneasiness stemmed, in part, from reports that high officials in
China's Government, anxious for Russia to remove her troops,
were willing to meet the new demands.

By January, 1902, the negotiations had reached the final stage.

The proposals provided for the evacuation of Russian troops providing no disturbance took place requiring their presence, a qualification of no minor importance. Further, there was a deeply disturbing clause. The proposed agreement called for the granting of a monopoly to the Russo-Chinese Bank for the financing of railway and mining enterprises in Manchuria.

It was at this time Secretary of State Hay crossed the line limiting U.S. protests to the defense of equality of commercial opportunity. On December 6, he wired Conger "to say to Prince Ch'ing that the President trusts and expects that no arrangement will be made with any single power which will permanently impair the territorial integrity of China or impair the ability of China to meet her international obligations." [20] It was not customary for Hay to speak directly of the President's wishes. One may speculate that, perhaps, the energetic Roosevelt was responsible for taking the stronger stand.

On February 1, 1902, Hay gave equally emphatic instructions. The proposed agreement between China and the Russo-Chinese Bank, caused Hay to instruct Conger to tell the Chinese: "Such monopoly would distinctly controvene treaties of China with foreign powers, affect rights of citizens of the United States by restricting rightful trade, and tend to impair sovereign rights of China and diminish her ability to meet international obligations." [21] It would, moreover, he warned, lead other nations to seek similar advantages in other parts of the Empire.

During the same month Great Britain and Japan signed an Alliance of great importance. In it, Great Britain agreed that should Japan be at war and a third power intervene against her, Great Britain would go to the aid of Japan. Conger had lunch with the British Minister, Sir Ernest Satow, on February 12. Satow recorded: "He thinks it the most important political event that has occurred for a long time, and that the Japanese could, if they were so-minded, turn out the Russians from Manchuria. He thinks it is a good thing that we have managed to prevent the Chinese signing the Manchurian convention and the agreement with the Russo-Chinese Bank, and hopes the United States will be able to come into line with us." [22] When Satow spoke to Prince Ch'ing about the Alliance, Ch'ing approved of it and said he thought it would facilitate the negotiations for Russia's evacuation of Manchuria.[23] At that same conference, Prince Ch'ing furnished Satow with a copy of the Manchurian Convention then being negotiated. Russia was prepared to agree to the restoration of Chinese authority in Manchuria and the withdrawal of Rusian troops in three stages. The other Russian requests were again held in abeyance.

On February 19, Satow saw Robert Hart, the Director of the Imperial Maritime Customs Service. Hart told him of a conversation he had recently had with a high Chinese official indicating Chinese uneasiness over the Alliance. It had, said the Chinese, "put China in the disagreeable position of having to take part and perhaps quarrel with the power from whom she had most to fear, namely, Russia. . . ." The Chinese official also asked if the agreement did not "leave it in the power of Japan to herself take possession of Manchuria if she succeeded in driving out the Russians."[24]

It is most interesting to note that during the final days of Russia's negotiations with China the British Minister, in dealing with Prince Ch'ing, was instructed as follows:

> It would be most desirable that the language of your American and Japanese colleagues to Chinese government should accord with yours, and you should confer with them to this end.[25]

The American Minister was also instructed to consult with his British and Japanese colleagues. An unusual degree of collaboration had been achieved between these Powers.

The Manchurian Convention, signed on April 8, 1902, providing simply for the evacuation of Russia's regular army troops, failed to reduce the tensions and Russia's moves continued to stir unrest. In the same month, Henry B. Miller, Consul in Newchwang, made a trip through Manchuria going as far north as Harbin. On his return he gave Conger an account of the business activities of the Russians outside of the treaty ports, testified to the determination of the Russians to continue doing business wherever they pleased, and warned that the Anglo-Japanese Alliance would not deter Russia. She will, predicted Miller, be "more modest in appearance and more circumspect in methods, but will continue to press all enterprises here." He urged the sending of more American Consuls and the opening of more treaty ports as a way to counteract the Russians.[26]

The persistency of the watch the United States maintained over Russia in Manchuria was not matched by a similar surveillance over activities of other nations. On May 14, 1902, Conger reported that Great Britain and China had signed two agreements relating to the return of the Peking-Shanhaikwan Railway to China. Great Britain had held this railway since the Boxer Revolt, with the understanding that she would relinquish it at the conclusion of the Peking Conference and the evacuation of the troops of the Allied Expedition. She now insisted on the Powers giving their consent to the two agreements before carrying out her promise. Conger noted that there was no possibility of all the Powers giving their consent as the net effect would be the perpetuation of British control. The first agreement required China to retain a British Military Codirector and German and Japanese Subdirectors. The second agreement prohibited any new foreign-owned railway line within a distance of eighty miles of the Peking-Shanhaikwan Railway.[27]

Conger thought the British object was to keep Russia out of the area and that British retention of the railway would cause the Russians to leave their troops in Manchuria. He also expressed concern over the impact on Americans who were seeking mining concessions in the area. If they succeeded in gaining these concessions, they would wish to build railways to move the ore.

However, the major importance of Conger's response lies in his reason for giving his consent to the first agreement. He wrote to Hay:

> While I think the railway should be turned over absolutely to the Chinese, yet I have concluded that under the policy practiced by the United States since the arrival of the allied forces, and my general instructions, I ought not to object to the agreement, and shall, therefore, give my assent to Agreement "A".[28]

Hay immediately cabled his approval.[29] Cooperation with Great Britain took precedence over minor differences between the two countries. The United States placed a higher priority on cooperating with Great Britain than she did on adherence to abstract principle. The traditional policy against alliances did not inhibit collaboration.

The alignment of the United States on the side of Great Britain and Japan vis-à-vis Russia in Manchuria did not involve any commitment to joint action. A common interest had led to a considerable degree of consultation and mutual understanding. However, neither national interests nor national attitudes toward foreign policy questions in the United States permitted more than parallel, as opposed to joint, action with Great Britain and Japan. Even this course, followed with caution, soon led into the labyrinth of Asian politics.

The negotiation of a new commercial treaty with China served as the entryway. At the Peking Conference of Ministers following the Boxer holocaust, China agreed to enter into discussions of new treaties. Great Britain and Japan led the way, and their negotiations were well along when John Hay, on January 21, 1902, instructed Conger to open negotiations. Hay informed Conger that he should be guided by the Secretary's letter to Rockhill, dated April 11, 1901. In this letter Hay stated: "Essential object is to favor Chinese financial stability and promote ability to buy in any market and to exchange native products wherever produced on equal terms with all nations." Hay also expressed his hope for the abolition of likin, the internal tax, and at the same time an increase in duties "so as to add to China's revenue." "These duties," said Hay, "should not be the same on all imports." "Lower duties should be attached to imports tending to develop China's productiveness," he wrote. He thought agricultural implements and the simpler type of manufacturing machinery should be favored. Conger was instructed to sound out his colleagues on these points.[30]

At this stage, Hay made no mention of asking China to open new treaty ports in Manchuria. This demand was added later in the negotiations and by April, 1903, it had become the major issue in relations between the United States and Russia.

Many high officials of the Russian Government looked forward to reducing Manchuria to a client state.[31] As early as September, 1902, the Governor of the Amur region, wrote to Kuropatkin that Russia was using "the existing historical course of events, to create out of Manchuria the autonomous state with a vassal dependence upon Russia similar to Bukhara or Khiva."[32] Not all Russian officials went as far as this, but some form of Russian dominance was generally agreed upon.

The American demand to open treaty ports in Manchuria challenged the Russian program. The opening of the cities plus a commitment to adhere to Hay's principles of equality of commercial opportunity would, in all probability, deprive Russia of some of the fruits of commerce while she bore all the cost of administration and development.[33] Russia faced other dangers if the new cities were to be opened to foreign residence. In this event it was quite likely that the cities would be inundated with Japanese immigrants. Were this to take place not only would Manchuria be lost to Russia but she would face a threat to her maritime provinces.

If the policy-makers in Washington recognized the basis of Russian opposition, they left no written records to this effect. In fact, the records suggest they attributed the whole Russian case to deceit and trickery. They adamantly pursued their aim of opening the treaty ports. Cassini, the Russian Ambassador, recognized the iron-willed determination of the Americans and advised his Government that there was a possibility of "most serious decisions from the side of the United States in a sense of a direct entente with Japan and England."[34]

In Washington, the negotiations were conducted by Rockhill, who had recently returned from Peking where he had served as the U.S. representative during the Boxer negotiations. He had concluded that Russia was intent on taking over Manchuria. He and John Hay found that while Russia did not openly oppose the opening of two cities in Manchuria, she was, in fact, doing her best to prevent China from granting the request.

The negotiations gave rise to a lively hostility. In April, 1903, Rockhill received reports that Russia had threatened China with a refusal to evacuate her troops from Manchuria if she agreed to open the two cities to foreign trade.[35] This led Hay to question Cassini. Hay gave his report of the interview to Roosevelt: "He pretended to know nothing whatever about the convention, but discussed it point by point in a manner so clear and minute as if he had written it himself."[36] The Russian Foreign Minister similarly told the American Ambassador that he had no knowledge of any demands upon China. Then, the following day Conger cabled from Peking that the Russian Chargé d'Affaires had repeated the demands on China. Hay concluded that "dealing with a government with whom mendacity is a science is an extremely difficult and delicate matter." Cassini, in turn, warned that Hay was indignant, that he had charged that Russia was placing his Government in a completely untenable situation, and that for several days Hay threatened joint action with Great Britain and Japan.[37] However, Hay held out hope that St. Petersburg would repudiate its representative in Peking. In that case, wrote Hay, he would be willing to forget. "We are not charged with the cure of the Russian soul, and we may let them go to the devil at their own sweet will."[38]

Rockhill persisted in his efforts to have Russia withdraw her opposition. She did so on July 14 after the Russian Ambassador in Washington was assured that the United States had no intention of demanding that the two cities be opened to settlement.[39] When China then said she would only open the two cities after Russia had withdrawn her troops, Washington took a firm position with Peking. On August 13, China agreed to the American demands and on October 8 the new commercial treaty was signed. It included an article providing for the opening of Antung and Mukden to foreign trade. This concession amounted to little for the treaty did not specify a date for the opening of the ports nor that they would be open to foreign residents. The Russians were readily able to accept such a version.

Negotiations between the United States and Russia on the question of opening the two cities in Manchuria were still in process when Japan, on July 3, 1903, sent a series of proposals to St. Petersburg for the settlement of the Manchurian and Korean issues between the two countries. These clearly portended a showdown. While these negotiations concerned Russia and Japan primarily, Great Britain, under the Alliance, was fully informed. The United States did not participate directly. Roosevelt and Hay continued to affirm that the United States adhered to "an independent course." While this affirmation was not directly contradicted by the actions of the President and Secretary of State, they hovered uncertainly between the role of observer and participant.

Japan was obligated to keep Great Britain informed and she was careful to do so. Her Ambassador in London, Hayashi, met with the British Foreign Minister Lord Lansdowne on July 3. Lansdowne, at the conclusion of their discussion, said that he thought it was "most important that we should endeavor to arrive at an understanding with the United States in regard to the action which they would be likely to adopt in dealing with these questions."[40] Hayashi responded that his Government did not wish to do so.[41] Until late in the negotiations Japan adhered to this view. Lansdowne, however, did not change his opinion even though he honored Japan's wishes. In a conference with Joseph Choate, the U.S. Ambassador, Lansdowne, according to the Ambassador's report, took the occasion to say:

> that while he knew and appreciated the disposition of our Government not to take any joint action in such matters, yet that where our interests were identical as in the matter of trade with Manchuria, he thought our common (interests) would be promoted by keeping each other fully informed as to what we were doing, so as to keep in touch with each other.[42]

Choate replied that such an exchange would certainly meet with the wishes of Secretary of State Hay.

On the basis of the written records of the conversations between American and Japanese representatives during the following months it can only be concluded that Japan did not keep Washington fully informed. However, Japan changed course in December, 1903.[43]

In the meantime, the difficulties standing in the way of a settlement became more visible. On July 24, Conger wrote to Hay giving him a report of the views expressed by Russia's Minister in Peking, Pavel Lessar. Conger summed up his views:

> Mr. Lessar frankly says that there are only two things that the Russians can do; they must either annex Manchuria, or they must make some arrangement whereby they can withdraw and leave the Chinese their active and sympathetic friends. If they were to withdraw without such an arrangement, it would take a very large army to protect their railway and other interests there, and Russia would thus, at her own expense, be policing and keeping in order an extensive and unfriendly country for the benefit of the trade and interests of the rest of the world.[44]

Given this situation, Lessar thought it would be wiser "to annex, and police and restrain only for themselves."

Lessar's opinion cannot be ascribed to the Russian Government but in December and January, the positions taken by the Ministry for Foreign Affairs clearly delineated the Russian dilemma. The Czar, the Minister for Foreign Affairs, and the diplomatic representatives abroad wished to avoid war, but the military favored taking a stand so strong that war was the only possibility. Insofar as these two groups were able to reach agreement, they opposed a treaty with Japan or any country other than China regarding the future of Manchuria.[45] They were willing to offer assurances to the other nations having treaty rights in Manchuria that these would not be disturbed. However, they hedged this about with the stipulation that this assurance "was given without prejudice to the conditions which might in the future finally determine the relations of Russia with Manchuria."[46] Russia similarly insisted, with great emphasis, on excluding the right to establish settlements.[47] Hayashi told Lansdowne that the latter constituted a most dangerous limitation. It was, said Hayashi, "evidently intended to condemn them (Japan) for all time to live in other parts of that province (other than Newchwang) on sufferance under a virtually Russian Government."[48]

This question of foreign settlements in Manchuria brought the United States into the discussion. Japan contended that as another Power (the United States) had been promised that China would open two more cities in Manchuria, Japan should enjoy the same rights.[49] However, Russia remained adamant. The French Ambassador in London informed Lansdowne on January 19 that M. Delcasse, the French Minister for Foreign Affairs, "did not think Russian Government, although ready to go to great lengths in the direction of the open door in Manchuria, would be likely to give way on a question of right of settlement—it was not objected to as far as European Powers were concerned, but if granted to Japanese would mean their swarming over Manchuria."[50]

Two days later, on January 21, the British Minister to Russia, Charles Scott, advised Lansdowne that he thought that the question of the settlements was now less important. He based this on a statement of Japan's Minister in St. Petersburg, Shinichiro Kurino. The latter had told him that the U.S. Minister in Tokyo, Lloyd Griscom, had given him an explanation of the provision in the U.S. treaty with China providing for the opening of Mukden and Antung. This explanation, said Scott, had made the question of the settlements less important.[51]

Hay's instructions to Griscom on this point are significant. While the United States did not waive the right to select sites for residence and trade at Mukden and Antung, nevertheless "it did not ask at present for the establishment of such settlements at either locality, our trade interests not requiring them. . . ."[52] On January 13, Griscom was informed by the Japanese Government that it concurred in the view of the United States.[53]

The explanation of the United States reflected the cautious mood of the Department of State as war approached. Whether inspired by timidity in the face of war, or by thoughtfulness when faced by a degree of responsibility for having pushed the Manchurian issue, Secretary of State Hay clearly wished to avoid any move that could be interpreted as encouraging hostilities. It was this mood that led to thought of mediation. There are regrettable gaps in the written records dealing with proposals to mediate but what transpired can be, at least in part, reconstructed.

Lloyd Griscom, on December 8, informed Hay of Japan's concern about the posture of the United States. Japan's Foreign Minister expressed regret over the withdrawal of the American fleet to Honolulu. He also told Griscom that Japan hoped that the United States would "do something about our (the United States) newly acquired treaty ports." Griscom noted: "I gave him no encouragement, not knowing what is intended. . . . I am giving them no handle to draw us in."[54]

There were those who thought that the United States should take the lead and, with the support of Great Britain and France, seek to have the dispute between Russia and Japan referred to the Hague Tribunal. On December 18, the British Cabinet discussed the possibility of mediation. Lansdowne wanted Great Britain "to try its hand as a mediator" and to enlist the help of the United States. The Cabinet voted down the proposal.[55] Japan feared efforts at mediation and made this clear to Lansdowne and to Hay.[56] The Japanese argued that such an effort would consume many weeks and serve to give Russia time to prepare.

The position of the United States remained that of an observer. She fully shared the antipathy toward Russia, but had no intention of joining in the hostilities on the side of Japan. Nevertheless, when Sir Ernest Satow told Conger that Great Britain could never sit by and see Japan crushed, and that he did not think the United States would sit by, Conger gave an interesting reply. He observed, as reported by Satow, "that the present President is a man of courage and determination, who has always carried the country and Congress with him in whatever he has undertaken, and possibly he might think (sic) action to pressure United States commerce in Manchuria. Finance and commerce usually carry everything before them."[57]

In February, Japan went to war against Russia. During the early days of the conflict a friend wrote to Rockhill that the American Asiatic Association was blindly partisan to Japan and failed to view the Far Eastern scene from an American point of view. His friend recalled the friendly acts of Russia during the Civil War. Rockhill took the occasion to express his views on Russia.

> I must say that I don't attach much importance to the question of Russian friendship in 1863. Gratitude between nations is a poor thing to count on where material interests do not come in to strengthen it and keep it alive. We can still stand a certain amount of gratitude toward France, but trade and a certain similarity in our views on many subjects make it endurable. I don't see that the same reasons exist in the case of Russia. I don't think there is a nation on the face of the earth which has fewer points of contact, intellectually or in any other shape, with us than it.[58]

Theodore Roosevelt confided to his son that he was pro-Japanese.[59] No regrets entered his thinking. Compared to Lansdowne, who accepted the war reluctantly and whose correspondence reflects anxiety and a note of resentment against the overriding forces of history, Roosevelt was the epitome of composure.

Yet, while the United States had sided with Japan and Great Britain in opposing Russia, Hay had compromised with Russia on the question of the opening up of the cities in Manchuria and had abandoned his demands that foreign settlement should be allowed in them. He had, likewise, carefully avoided involvement in the war between Russia and Japan.

NOTES

1. A. Burlingame Johnson to Assistant Secretary of State David J. Hill, October 5, 1899. Hereafter consular dispatches cited are from the Department of State Archives.
2. *Ibid.*, March 5, 1900.
3. Witte, *Memoirs*, Part I, pp. 157, 163, cited by Anatoly Kantorovich, *Amerika v Bor'be za Kitae* (Moscow: State Social Economic Publishing House, 1935), p. 146.
4. Chester C. Tan, *The Boxer Catastrophe* (New York: Columbia University Press, 1955), p. 163.
5. Alvey A. Adee, Acting Secretary of State, to the representatives of the United States in Berlin, London, Paris, Rome, St. Petersburg, and Tokyo, August 29, 1900, *Papers Relating to the Foreign Relations of the United States, 1900,* pp. 304, 305. Hereafter cited as *U.S. Foreign Relations.*
6. Peirce, U.S. Chargé d'Affaires in St. Petersburg, to Adee, August 30, 1900, cited by Edward H. Zabriskie, *American–Russian Rivalry in the Far East: A Study in Diplomacy and Power Politics 1895–1914* (Philadelphia: University of Pennsylvania Press, 1946), p. 63.
7. *Ibid.*
8. Andrew Malozemoff, *Russian Far Eastern Policy 1881–1904: With Special Emphasis on the Causes of the Russo–Japanese War* (Berkeley: University of California Press, 1958), pp. 153–155; William Langer, *The Diplomacy of Imperialism 1890–1902* (2nd ed.; New York: Alfred A. Knopf, 1951), p. 712; and Tan, pp. 165–167.
9. Langer, pp. 714–716.
10. *Ibid.*, p. 719.
11. Zabriskie, p. 69.
12. Secretary of State John Hay to Foreign Office, Tokyo, February 1, 1901, cited by Zabriskie, p. 69.
13. A. L. P. Dennis, *Adventures in American Diplomacy 1896–1906* (New York: E. P. Dutton & Co.), p. 243.
14. Boris A. Romanov, *Rossia v Mandrzliurei, 1892–1906* (Leningrad: Izdanie Leningradskogo Vostochnogo Institutaimeni A. S. Enukidze, 1928), p. 304, cited by Zabriskie, p. 71.
15. Tan, pp. 187–188.

16. *Ibid.*, p. 189.

17. *Ibid.*, pp. 192–193.

18. Hay to Conger, August 29, 1901.

19. *Ibid.*, November 14, 1901.

20. *Ibid.*, December 6, 1901.

21. *Ibid.*, February 1, 1902.

22. George Alexander Lensen (ed.), *Korea and Manchuria between Russia and Japan 1895–1914: The Observations of Sir Ernest Satow* (Tallahassee, Florida: The Diplomatic Press, 1966), p. 172.

23. *Ibid.*, p. 173.

24. *Ibid.*, p. 177.

25. *Ibid.*, p. 180.

26. Henry B. Miller, Consul in Newchwang, to Conger, April 30, 1902.

27. Conger to Hay, May 14, 1902; Conger to Hay, May 15, 1902.

28. *Ibid.*

29. Hay to Conger, May 15, 1902.

30. Hay to Conger, January 21, 1902.

31. At a meeting of four Ministers of the Russian Government on October 31, 1902, it was unanimously agreed that "there is no doubt in the future, that Manchuria will have to be annexed to Russia, or put in the full dependence from her," but against the insistence of Witte who thought it necessary "to leave the accomplishment of this process to a historical course of events. . . ." Kuropatkin differed with Witte, arguing "that the longer we will postpone the solution consistent with Russian interests, the harder it will be to execute this decision. . . ." Report of Conference of October 31, 1902, Archives of Ministry for Foreign Affairs, cited by Kantorovich, p. 146.

32. Gradekov to Kuropatkin, September 24, 1902, Archives of Ministry for Foreign Affairs, cited by Kantorovich, p. 146. Walter Townley, British Chargé d'Affaires in Peking in 1903, in the absence of Sir Ernest Satow, sent home a translation of a Russian note explaining her position. It read:

> Russia and China have for more than 200 years had with each other relations that have been always distinguished by their very friendly character, and this very naturally—two neighboring people, having a common frontier more than 5,000 versts in length, and many common affairs and interests, may easily come to an understanding about everything. . . .
>
> This applies particularly to Manchuria. Russia has sacrificed thousands of lives and millions of treasure for the pacification of this country and for the restoration in it of lawful Chinese authority quite apart from the millions that have been expended in the construction of a great railway for the commercial benefit of all nations. Other powers have not expended on the pacification of Manchuria a single rouble or a single soldier. It would seem, therefore, full just that Russia should have the right to safeguard her interests, bought at so

high a price, in that country, without waking the jealousy of other powers.
Walter Townley to Lansdowne, No. 173, Peking, May 4, 1903, F.O. 405–134, pp. 202–204, cited by Lensen, p. 214. .

33. This view was expressed by Russia's Minister in Peking, Pavel Lessar, in a report written in 1903. He wrote: ". . . the United States do not make it a secret, that with securing of 'open doors' in Manchuria, they even would like us to take upon ourselves the sacrifices and expenses to assure that order would be upheld in the area, which would promote the development of the commerce of other countries. But endless occupation can scarcely be accomplished; and we could satisfy the cabinet in Washington only by granting permission to import foreign goods into Manchuria, which would be annexed to our territory, according to a tariff which would be the same to us as to others, and not to exceed the existing Chinese tariff. Under such conditions, this area would be acquisition of doubtful value to us." A report of Lessar of June 4, 1903, accompanied by a note of Nicholas II entitled "Many Useful Thoughts," cited by Kantorovich, p. 154.

34. Cassini to Lamsdorf, June 10, 1903, Archives of Ministry for Foreign Affairs, cited by Kantorovich, p. 150.

35. *U. S. Foreign Relations, 1903*, p. 53.

36. Hay to Roosevelt, April 28, 1903, Hay Papers, Library of Congress.

37. Lamsdorf to Cassini, June 22, 1903, Archives of Ministry for Foreign Affairs, cited by Kantorovich, p. 150.

38. Hay to Roosevelt, May 12, 1903, Hay Papers.

39. Payson J. Treat, *Diplomatic Relations between the United States and Japan 1895–1905* (Stanford: Stanford University Press, 1938), p. 186.

40. Lansdowne to Sir Claude MacDonald, July 3, 1903, *The Anglo–Japanese Alliance and the Franco–British Entente*, Vol. II: *British Documents on the Origins of the War 1898–1914* (London: His Majesty's Stationery Office, 1927), p. 207, hereafter cited as *British Documents*.

41. *Ibid.*

42. Choate to Hay, July 18, 1903, cited by Dennis, p. 359.

43. Treat, p. 179.

44. Conger to Hay, July 24, 1903, Hay Papers, cited by Dennis, p. 381.

45. Sir C. Scott to Lansdowne, December 28, 1903, *British Documents*, II, 227.

46. Lansdowne to MacDonald, January 11, 1904, *ibid.*, 233.

47. *Ibid.*

48. *Ibid.*

49. Lansdowne to MacDonald, January 14, 1904, Enclosure, Instructions to the Japanese Minister in St. Petersburg, *British Documents*, II, 233–234; Treat, p. 183.

50. Lansdowne to Scott, January 19, 1904, *British Documents*, II, 237.

51. Scott to Lansdowne, January 21, 1904, *ibid.*, 238–239.

52. Hay to Griscom, January 18, 1904, Dispatches to U.S. Minister to Japan, cited by Treat, pp. 185–186.

53. Treat, p. 184.

54. Griscom to Hay, December 8, 1903, Hay Papers, cited by Dennis, p. 385.

55. Ian Nish, *The Anglo–Japanese Alliance: The Diplomacy of Two Island Empires, 1894–1907* (London: The Athlone Press, 1966), p. 274.

56. Lansdowne to MacDonald, January 5, 1904, *British Documents*, II, 229; Treat, p. 182.

57. Lensen, p. 257.

58. Rockhill to F. B. Forbes, March 9, 1904, Rockhill Papers, Harvard University Library.

59. "I am greatly interested in the Russian and Japanese war. It has certainly opened most disastrously for the Russians, and their supine carelessness is well-nigh incredible. For several years Russia had behaved very badly in the Far East, her attitude toward all nations, including us, but especially toward Japan, being grossly overbearing. We had no sufficient cause for war with her. Yet, I was apprehensive lest if she at the very outset whipped Japan on the sea she might assume a position well-nigh intolerable toward us. I thought Japan might whip her on the sea, but I could not be certain; and between ourselves—for you must not breathe it to anybody—I was thoroughly well pleased with the Japanese victory, for Japan is playing our game." Theodore Roosevelt to Theodore Roosevelt, Jr., February 10, 1904, in Elting E. Morison (ed.), *The Square Deal, 1903–1905*, Vol. IV: *The Letters of Theodore Roosevelt* (Cambridge: Harvard University Press, 1951), p. 724.

CHAPTER VI

REVOLUTIONARIES IN SILK

MANY AMERICANS maintained that Japan, in her war with Russia, was fighting their battle. However understandable this view was, the results of the war altered the balance of power in East Asia in a way that was not wholly in harmony with the long-term interests of the United States.

Japan emerged more powerful than Russia had been prior to the war. Unlike Russia, she did not have a border in Europe to defend and she could concentrate her forces in one area and in close proximity to home. Second, the Japanese took over the extensive Russian rights in southern Manchuria, including two leaseholds, a major railroad, and the many privileges which went with these. While Russia had been weak at sea, Japan had a powerful fleet. In addition, Japan was allied to Great Britain, the only nation that could challenge her at sea.

The problem of the United States was further complicated by the weakness of China. Rockhill, shortly after his arrival in Peking as Minister, wrote:

> The lack of any settled policy among the high officers of the Chinese Government, I refrain from using the word statesman as I fear there is not one to be found in China at the present day, is terribly evident. Indecision and a determination to drift with any current is shown on every side. It is manifest to the most casual observer that China is quite unable to manage her international affairs without strong support and constant pressure from without.[1]

China's weakness stood as an invitation to powerful nations to exploit her resources without the restraints that only a strong government in Peking could have imposed.

The depth of the humiliation turned both the Manchus and the Chinese toward change. These new national aspirations did not escape the attention of American diplomatic representatives but they failed to see that the Foreign Powers would eventually have to accept adjustments not to their liking. The movements under way were to have such dramatic effects on the world's relations with China that they are worthy of close attention even though they were only in their beginning.

The ruling Manchu Dynasty accepted the necessity of change but prefaced every move for reform with calculations as to how it could strengthen its own position by a greater centralization of power and at the same time not increase the influence of the Chinese in the central regime. It was the unrelenting pressure of the fiscal problem after 1905 that compelled the Manchus to try their hand at political innovations. The jungle-like system of taxation, the product of a thousand years of improvisation, no longer met the need for revenue. The revenue came from several types of taxation: tribute rice; land taxes paid in silver; the salt gabelle; duties on imports; likin; customs duties collected by the Imperial Maritime Customs Service; and contributions from the provinces for "Peking extras" and the expenses of the Imperial household.

The Central Government received about 2,090,000 hundred-weight of rice primarily from the provinces of Kiangsu and Chekiang. The rice was stored in granaries in Peking and used to pay officials and soldiers a part of their monthly stipend. The value of the grain was estimated at $3,684,240, but the cost of shipping the rice to Peking via the Grand Canal and by sea, an operation carried out by the government Grain Transport Service and involving some six thousand imperial grain junks and seventy thousand boatmen, was costly. The system, long since outdated, had been necessary centuries before when Peking first became the capital and when the northern region could not supply the food demanded by the Imperial household, the military garrison, and officialdom.[2]

The taxes on land yielded $18,339,328. Another $9,984,729 came from the salt monopoly and another $9,000,000 came from likin. In addition, the Imperial Maritime Customs Service collected some $16,074,178 for the Board of Revenue. Native customs produced another $731,000. Taxes on opium amounted to $629,399 and other miscellaneous taxes provided $4,020,500.

The total revenue of Peking in 1894 was thus estimated at $65,043,649.[3]

A British study prepared in the 1890's made two striking observations. Peking's income from land taxes was only half of that collected from the people. The remainder was held by local officials for their own use. Second, the Government of India, by the levying of almost identical taxes collected $73,100,000 compared to China's $18,339,328; the salt tax in India brought in $24,123,000 while China's netted only $9,984,729.[4]

The limited income of Peking had met government expenses prior to the war with Japan in 1894–1895, but it then became grossly inadequate. At the close of that war, China's indebtedness reached $58,398,000. The indemnity to Japan added another $168,130,000. To meet this debt, she negotiated two foreign loans of $73,100,000 each. Commenting on the problem China faced, Minister Charles Denby, in 1897, wrote, "To provide for even the interest on these sums is beyond the scope of China's present income."

This was only the sad prelude to the increase in government expenses during the next ten years. The Boxer indemnity alone was set at four hundred and fifty million taels or three hundred and thirty-three million dollars. Anxious to build a railway system that would provide a basis for a truly national government, Peking borrowed some £32,948,300 for this purpose in the years 1899 to 1911. At the close of 1911, the foreign indebtedness of the Chinese Government totaled £139,527,161.[5] The Chinese scholar, Shao-Kwan Chen, concluded that whereas the Government enjoyed a balance of 11,066,566 taels of revenue over expenditures in 1887, it faced a deficit of 41,689,573 taels in 1911.[6]

The financial problem and the whole array of difficulties faced by the Dynasty at the close of the Russo-Japanese War convinced the Empress Dowager that changes were necessary. The old civil service examinations were abolished, an extensive system of public education was launched, the beginnings of a modern army got under way, and the first steps were taken toward political reform. To prepare the way for a revamped government structure, a commission of five distinguished scholars was sent abroad to study western constitutional government. In 1906, various government boards were reshuffled. The commission, upon its return, recommended limiting the powers of the local Viceroys and Governors and outlined plans for a new constitution, one that would have greatly strengthened Imperial control while providing a Parliament that would serve as a facade.[7]

These conservative aims contrasted sharply with the liberal views of the Constitutional Party led by Liang Ch'i-ch'ao. In 1907, when Liang organized the Political Information Club, he presented a program that called for a cabinet responsible to Parliament, an independent judiciary, a clear-cut definition of the powers of both the central and local governments, and, finally, new political machinery for the effective conduct of diplomacy.[8] The party proposed to achieve these reforms through peaceful and orderly persuasion.

In 1907, the Constitutional Party believed that the Manchus could be moved to accept its program. When the Peking regime in 1908 called for the election of Provincial Assemblies, their hopes appeared to be confirmed. The announced aim was to prepare the way for popularly elected assemblies having legislative power. However, it soon became clear that the proposed assemblies were little more than a device of the Dynasty for winning approval for increased taxes.

The Assemblies were granted only advisory powers. A strictly limited suffrage based on educational and property qualifications was established. Only members of the professions, students, and those possessing property valued at five thousand dollars could vote.

Elections to these Provincial Assemblies in the summer of 1909 ranged from unseemly buying and selling of votes in the Canton area to elections with respectable voter participation, free from corruption.[9] The Assemblies were dominated by the gentry. Of the one hundred and twenty-seven elected in Szechwan, almost all held a degree, approximately twenty-five held official ranks, and nine were listed as "famously wealthy."[10] The assemblies elected in Shantung and Fengtien had approximately ninety-five and eighty-seven percent degree holders.[11] While statistics are not available for all of the provinces, it appears that the Constitutionalists held a majority and very few Revolutionaries won seats.

The elections, Charles Tenney, Secretary of the U.S. Legation, reported, excited no popular enthusiasm. "Generally speaking," he said, "owing to the high qualifications of electors and owing to the close control of the officials over the elections, the common people seem to look upon these first provincial assemblies as new parts of the governmental machinery rather than as bodies representing the people, though certain exceptions must be made to this general statement." Tenney considered most of them to be docile, but he also approved of their moderation and dignity. He was optimistic about their future: "There is a strong spirit of democracy among the people with which the nominally despotic government has always had to reckon and that spirit will cause the people to make good use of the new parliamentary machinery when they come to understand it better." [12]

Instructions from Peking to the Assemblies forbade discussion of foreign affairs, but security against foreign domination was foremost in everyone's mind. By 1910, there was further general unrest due to the debasing of the coinage and the consequent decline in the purchasing power of wage earners. But as one American representative explained, "the phase most in evidence to Consuls is political,—the feeling that the Chinese should regain what they believe to be their lost rights." The weakness of the Peking Government and the "China for the Chinese" cry, with students at the bottom of it, dominated public discussion.[13]

The resolutions adopted by the Provincial Assembly of Fukien, meeting in Foochow, resounded with resentment against the foreigner. The Foreign Ministers in Peking were called upon "to revise the regulations of the Kulangsu International Settlement so that the interests of Chinese living on Kulangsu may be better guarded." A second resolution demanded that foreigners be stopped from acquiring land in nontreaty ports. The Assembly pointed to the evasion of treaty provisions by the Standard Oil Company in acquiring land about one hundred miles north of Amoy. The installation of storage tanks, declared the Assembly, endangered the lives of the people. A third resolution called for a prohibition against foreign signboards outside of treaty ports. A fourth urged "that all persons of Chinese birth who have taken on foreign naturalization be deprived of the rights and privileges of Chinese citizens in non-treaty ports." A fifth resolution declared that all foreigners traveling in the interior without proper passports stamped by the local officials or their respective Consuls be arrested. A final resolution demanded that missionaries not be permitted to erect houses and other buildings in the interior until their title deeds had been investigated and stamped and not until it was determined that there was no objection on the part of the local Self-Government Society, Tgu Chih Hui.[14]

Charles Tenney visited several of the Assemblies. He found the Hunan and Hupeh Assemblies showing the most independent spirit. Tenney reported: "They voiced the sentiment of the provincial gentry in making most emphatic protests against the foreign railway loans and showed a disposition to oppose the officials in a way that caused some disquietude to the latter." [15] Brownell Gage of the Yale Mission at Changsha wrote that the Honan Assembly had decided that "foreigners are not to be allowed to buy any more land in the province." This was, wrote Gage, contrary to the treaties, "but the Hunanese do not seem to mind that." [16]

The Kiangsu Assembly, meeting in Nanking in 1909, touched upon the questions arising out of Japanese businessmen's activities in the area. When the Assembly met the second time in 1910, three questions occupied the major attention: the circulation of foreign paper notes, taxes on land titles held by foreigners, and the amount of foreign bank notes in circulation. "In putting our notes into circulation," said the Assembly, "our object is to restore China's sovereign rights as viewed from a financial standpoint." Likewise, the delegates resolved, "The clandestine establishment of their (foreigners) firms and stores in the interior not only hinders native business but occasions controversies between one nation and another." Therefore, the Assembly requested "that prompt measures be taken to interdict such actions (on the part of the Japanese) and to communicate with the Consul, with a view that his nationals be instructed to remove from the interior. . . ." [17]

These efforts in the Provincial Assemblies did not satisfy the revolutionary T'ung-meng Hui led by Dr. Sun Yat-sen. The T'ung-meng Hui, which had its headquarters in Tokyo, carried on its activities secretly and made every effort to win converts in the army and did so with success. It likewise exploited the opportunities presented by famines and economic hardship in any form, although it did not make a direct appeal to the peasants.[18]

The main support for the T'ung-meng Hui came from students overseas and from those who had returned to China after study abroad. In 1906, in Tokyo alone, there were fifteen thousand Chinese students. It was in Tokyo in September, 1905, that Sun organized the society. The society's monthly newspaper, *The People*, enjoyed a circulation of approximately one hundred and fifty thousand. A year after its establishment, the society had ten thousand members in China.[19] In the years 1906 through 1908, the T'ung-meng Hui launched five attempts to overthrow the Dynasty by force and participated in two others.

Economic hardships and famines in 1909 and 1910 played into the hands of the revolutionaries. In 1909, districts of Honan were devastated by floods and the rice crop was in large part destroyed. Hupeh likewise suffered crop failures and much of the rice it did produce was exported. Refugees from the country districts flocked into the city of Changsha. These unfortunates confronted disaster. The gentry had secured possession of most of the available rice and then held it for speculative purposes. Early in April, 1909, the price rose to ten thousand cash per picul, five times the normal figure. On the night of April 13, a crowd gathered to demand relief. Representatives of the Provincial Governor announced that the price of rice was reasonable and then ordered the people to disperse.[20]

This arbitrary treatment led to revolt. After killing the police taotai a crowd moved against the Governor's yamen. Only the presence of troops saved the Governor. The crowd then set out to attack the missionaries knowing that the Governor would face serious difficulties if foreign governments charged him with failure to provide protection. Missionary properties were destroyed. The missionaries escaped with their lives by retreating to foreign ships on the nearby river. On the following day, under new leadership provided by "well dressed men, some with silk garments," the crowd again attacked the mission stations and then the rice shops, stores dealing in foreign goods, the Custom House, the Japanese Consulate, and all foreign business houses. The outburst ended with the looting of the Standard Oil and Asiatic Petroleum Companies.[21]

In the spring of 1910, a similar outbreak occurred in Suchien. A crop failure led to famine and the officials did nothing to relieve the distress. The people threatened to destroy the local flour mills unless the grain stored there was released at a reasonable price. The local magistrate, in placards posted throughout the town, was charged with accepting bribes from the owners of the mills. The controversy led to an attack on some local granaries, the looting of the homes of the rich and finally to the burning of the flour mills.[22]

Yet other disturbances took place in the provinces of Yunnan and Shantung; and in Tientsin, at a mass meeting in memorial of the tenth anniversary of the western allies capture of the city, one of the speakers warned: "Today, we meet to commemorate the loss of Tientsin ten years ago; in another ten years, we will meet to commemorate the loss of China." [23]

Early in 1910, an American business representative, Edward S. Little, reported to the American Legation what he had seen on his travels. Wherever he traveled, he wrote, the one subject of conversation was the foreign threat. A widely distributed publication predicted that China was to be carved up by the Foreign Powers during the coming spring. This had aroused students and converted them into "a noisy, irresponsible, and fiery class." In many provinces, Peking's failure to take a strong stand against foreign control of railways had deprived the Central Government of all control. He informed the Legation that societies were being formed to raise subscriptions for three national objects: the paying off of all foreign loans and indemnities, the building of a navy, and the construction of railways. In Hupeh, there were mass meetings on Sunday afternoons where every effort was made to have the people buy railway shares and to arouse them against foreign control. Wherever he went in the cities, there were now newspapers and all of them were "engaged in spreading the doctrine of hatred of the foreigner." [24]

The unrest of the summer of 1910 coincided with protests against the conservative nature of the Constitutional Assembly which was scheduled to meet for the first time that autumn. The Dynasty, it seemed, had done everything possible to assure itself of a docile session. Of the two hundred members, half were chosen by the Throne and the other half by the Provincial Assemblies, but the assembly nominees were subject to approval by the Governors-General of the provinces. In May, the Throne had announced its choice of members. The list included fourteen Imperial Princes and nobles, twelve Chinese and Manchu nobles, fourteen princes and nobles of the outer dependencies, six Imperial clansmen, and ten distinguished scholars. Another thirty-two had been chosen from one hundred and sixty nominees of the various government boards.[25]

A protest against the unrepresentative character of the membership of the Assembly was presented to the Prince Regent. It was signed by nominees of the Provincial Assemblies, members of the Bureau of Trade, many officeholders, members of Constitutional Reform Societies, and Chinese residing abroad. The Prince Regent denounced the protest and ordered an end to further agitation.

However, when the Assembly met, it immediately demonstrated a surprisingly independent spirit by adopting a resolution calling for an early convocation of Parliament. The U.S. Minister, William J. Calhoun, called this action "the most significant event in the history of China for the last half century." "The resolution," he reported, "was adopted by a rising vote amid great enthusiasm and cheering." The conservatives, said Calhoun, "seemed to be completely overawed."

Calhoun was alert to the implications for the dollar diplomacy of Taft and Knox. In writing to the Secretary of State, he warned:

> Financial reform, inquiry as to terms and applications of loans and to collection and use of public revenues are supposed to be the inspiration of the movement. It is in such an atmosphere that present loan negotiations are being conducted.[26]

When the Prince Regent issued an edict calling for the first meeting of Parliament to take place in 1913, the Assembly threatened to resign.[27] The Assembly had made a strong impression on those favoring reform. A small minority from the central and southern provinces had with skill and determination carried all before them and even the nobles in the Assembly had applauded the general condemnation of corruption and financial disaster.[28] So far, the outlook was for a peaceful transition to a new order.

The U.S. Minister watched these developments with approval but he also made the perceptive observation that "the difficulty will arise after the convocation of Parliament and its conscious inadequacy of being able to meet the situation without having recourse to methods which would attack every vested interest in the Empire." "The Crown appointees in the Senate," he wrote, "are now perfectly willing to join in platonic indictments of corruption." [29]

The refusal to call Parliament into session at once set in motion a wave of protest. New memorials made their way from the provinces. In Mukden, meetings attended by students, gentry, and merchants, passed resolutions urging the early opening of Parliament and the Viceroy agreed to forward the petition by telegraph. When the petition was rejected, another meeting was called. Fred Fisher, the U.S. Consul-General in Mukden, reported: "During the meeting, two students got up, took out knives from their pockets and inflicted severe wounds upon their own persons, and with their blood wrote upon white flags the four characters. . . ." ("Please open the Parliament"). On December 6, 1910, a crowd of twenty thousand marched to the Government Building and the Viceroy promised to submit a further memorial to the Throne.[30]

Late in April of 1911, two violent outbreaks took place in the South, one of them at Canton. A revolutionary assassinated the local Viceroy. Later in the month, about a hundred revolutionaries launched an assault on the Viceroy's yamen and engaged several thousand government troops. Forty-three of the rebels were killed and the twenty-three who were captured were executed. Their martyrdom led hundreds of young people to join the movement.[31]

The question of foreign control was central to the agitation immediately preceding the outbreak of revolution in Wuhan in October, 1911. The Hukuang loans by a consortium of foreign bankers early that year, the new alliance of Japan and Russia in the summer of 1910, and then the Imperial decree of May 13, 1911, proclaiming nationalization of railroads aroused great fear. Chinese in the provinces strongly opposed nationalization of the railways. The Director of Railways, Sheng Hsuan-huai, was widely known as corrupt and unscrupulous. Any extension of his projects offered no hope of either honest or efficient management. Moreover, the nationalization of railroads represented another step by the Manchus in their drive to centralize political, economic, and military control. This alone would have sufficed to arouse strong opposition, but the Manchus' willingness to borrow abroad in order to buy the railways strengthened the opposition. The willingness of the Dynasty to negotiate foreign loans was widely attributed to a desire to ward off financial disaster and at the same time to privately enrich itself.

The railway issue came to a head in Szechwan in the summer of 1911. The gentry in that province had long held the lead in demanding control of local railways, and they had purchased shares in the projected Szechwan-Hankow line.[32] When the gentry learned that the Dynasty had negotiated a foreign loan to finance the construction, they organized railway protection clubs.[33] In August, the Imperial Government ordered the Governor-General of Hupeh to lead troops to Szechwan to suppress the movement. He promptly marched to the scene of the protests and arrested the leaders. Fighting then broke out between the regular troops and the militia. The revolution against the Manchus moved forward with speed. The Manchu Dynasty collapsed almost at once. In February, 1912, the new Republic of China came into being.

The importance of the issue of foreign control and exploitation in the movement that led to the establishment of the Chinese Republic made little impact on the Department of State. Only observers on the scene sensed the depth of Chinese feelings. The China policy of the United States continued as before and failed to take into consideration that a major change had taken place whereby loyalty to the Dynasty was being replaced by loyalty to the State.

The failure to take this into account is attributable in part to a lack of previous experience with national revolutions in colonial areas and in part to the illusion that China's pathway to modernization lay in the development of foreign commerce and the adoption of western religious ideals. Americans continued to feel friendly to the Chinese in the years after the Russo-Japanese War, but their friendship was still of a paternalistic type, unable to embrace the aspirations of the Chinese.

NOTES

1. Rockhill to Hay, July 1, 1905, Department of State Archives.
2. Charles Denby to Secretary of State John Sherman, July 8, 1897. In this letter, Denby gives a detailed summary of the report by the British Consul, George Jamieson, entitled *Revenue and Expenditure of the Chinese Empire.*
3. *Ibid.*
4. *Ibid.*
5. Hosea Ballou Morse, *The Trade and Administration of China* (Shanghai: Kelly and Walsh, Limited, 1913), Appendix A, p. 411.
6. Shao-Kwan Chen, *The System of Taxation in China in the Tsing Dynasty, 1644–1911* ("Columbia University Studies in History, Economics and Public Law," LIX [New York: Columbia University Press, 1913]), 42–44.
7. For a good summary of these efforts at reform, *see* George M. Beckman, *The Modernization of China and Japan* (New York: Harper & Row, 1962), pp. 198–208.
8. Li Chien-nung, *The Political History of China 1840–1928*, trans. and ed. Ssu-yu Teng and Jeremy Ingalls (New York: D. Van Nostrand Co., 1956), p. 216.
9. Henry Fletcher to Secretary of State, January 21, 1910, Enclosure, Report by Charles Tenney. Microfilm copy in Records of the Department of State Relating to Internal Affairs of China, 1910–1929, Department of State Archives. Correspondence cited hereafter in this chapter is from source cited above unless otherwise noted.
10. Charles H. Hedtke, "The Genesis of Revolution in Szechwan," Paper delivered at the Hamsphere Conference (N.H.) in August, 1965. Copy available in Asian Library at the University of Michigan.
11. Chang Peng-yuan, "Constitutionalists and the Chinese Revolution of 1911," Paper delivered at the Hamsphere Conference in August, 1965. Copy available in Asian Library at the University of Michigan.
12. Fletcher to Secretary of State, January 21, 1910, Enclosure, Report by Charles Tenney.
13. Consul-General in Shanghai to Secretary of State, January 31, 1910.
14. Julian Arnold, Consul in Foochow, to Secretary of State, January 10, 1910.

15. Henry Fletcher to Secretary of State, January 21, 1910, Enclosure, Report by Charles Tenney.

16. Hubert Baugh, Vice-Consul-General in Hankow, to Assistant Secretary of State, January 25, 1910.

17. Albert Pontius, Vice-Consul in Nanking, to Secretary of State, May 12, 1910.

18. Yoshihiro Hatano, "Revolutionary Features of the Modernized Armies in the Late Ch'ing Period," Paper delivered at the Hamsphere Conference in August, 1965. Copy available in the Asian Library at the University of Michigan.

19. Beckman, pp. 208–212.

20. Hubert Baugh, Vice-Consul-General in Hankow, to Assistant Secretary of State, April 18, 1910.

21. *Ibid.*

22. Albert W. Pontius, Vice-Consul in Nanking, to Secretary of State, April 30, 1910.

23. William J. Calhoun, U.S. Minister to China, to Secretary of State, August 23, 1910.

24. Henry Fletcher to Secretary of State, March 5, 1910, Enclosure, Report by Edward S. Little in Shanghai, an American, to his firm Messrs. Brunner, Mond, & Co. on January 15, 1910.

25. W. J. Calhoun to Secretary of State, May 25, 1910, Enclosure, "Memorandum on the Chinese Constitutional Assembly by the Chinese Secretary."

26. *Ibid.*, October 25, 1910.

27. *Ibid.*

28. *Ibid.*, October 25, 1910.

29. *Ibid.*

30. Fred Fisher, Consul-General in Mukden, to Secretary of State, December 6, 1910.

31. *Ibid.*, p. 211.

32. Li Chien-nung, p. 242.

33. *Ibid.*, p. 243.

CHAPTER VII

AMERICAN IMAGES OF CHINA

Reform in China appealed to Americans who, with few exceptions, imagined a linear progression from the ancient culture to a democratic republic embodying all the virtues of the West. Within this field of vision existed important differences. The observers fell into three major groups. Within the business community, a small segment took a lively interest, but others scarcely took any notice of China. The better educated missionaries and a few scholars saw the China that was emerging in realistic terms and with considerable understanding of Chinese aspirations. Finally, there were the more sophisticated editors and journalists who, with the exception of those who were specialists on Asia, gave China only cursory attention.

Two major voices of the business community differed as to their interest in China. The *Commercial and Financial Chronicle,* a weekly published in New York, spoke for the sector interested in public utilities and railroads. The entire Far Eastern question penetrated its columns on only seven occasions between 1905 and 1910. Each time the editor addressed himself to topics of broad concern rather than the special problems of the business community in expanding trade.

When the Chinese launched a boycott of American goods in June, 1905, to protest the treatment of the Chinese in the United States and against the policy excluding all Chinese except the narrowly defined exempt classes, the *Commercial Chronicle* sided with the Chinese. The editor called the treatment of Chinese immigrants in the United States a disgrace. In the spring of 1906, he deplored the publicity about antiforeign disturbances in China and reminded those who predicted war that it was the white race and not the yellow race that went to war "for purposes of commercial advantage." [1] In 1908, when the House of Representatives questioned the return of the Boxer indemnity, the editor described the House as "a bumptious body with a good bit of narrow-minded selfishness when dealing with one it considers an inferior. . . ." [2] He commented in an offhand manner on the Knox Neutralization Proposal and rendered no opinion on its merits.[3] Clearly this publication did not consider China of sufficient importance to its readers to warrant an editorial policy.

In sharp contrast, the *Journal of Commerce,* an ardent advocate of reciprocal trade agreements and low tariffs, reported on international affairs around the world. This newspaper featured factual accounts of foreign commerce, careful analysis of the changing nature of American exports, and articles on economic developments in Europe and Asia. In traditional Whig fashion, it saw commerce as binding nations together and lessening the danger of war.

It reminded its readers with regularity that George Washington's Farewell Address no longer provided an adequate guide for the conduct of foreign relations. The United States, now a world power, must out of self-interest assume its rightful position. Indicative of the editor's views was his strong approval of the new alliances in Europe on the ground that they constituted a bulwark for peace.

The *Journal of Commerce* held China partly responsible for the difficulties of the situation in the Far East. In September, 1905, the editor wrote that now that Japan had defeated Russia and the threat of dismemberment no longer hung over China, "the nations that have stood for her integrity have some right to demand that she should cooperate with them to the extent of eliminating from her system of government, the venality, incapacity and ignorance. . . ." [4] It was the weakness of China that complicated Far Eastern diplomacy and that likewise inhibited the growth of trade.

The editor, on the other hand, condemned the U.S. policy on Chinese immigration. The treaty excluding Chinese, except merchants, students, and officials, expired in 1904 and the Chinese adamantly opposed its renewal. In the summer of 1905, the Chinese in the major coastal cities carried out a boycott of American goods. President Theodore Roosevelt sought to appease the

Chinese by ordering fair treatment by immigration authorities, but he also held fast to the position that Chinese laborers must not be admitted. In Peking, Rockhill exerted all possible pressure on the Government to suppress the boycott.

Long before the boycott movement got under way, the *Journal of Commerce* declared that the vision of a United States inundated by coolies was a trumped-up fear. There would be no great exodus of Chinese to the United States if the doors were completely open. One month before the issue reached a crisis due to the boycott, the editor termed the "conditions of admission of the exempt classes of Chinese immigrants so insulting and oppressive that no government with a particle of self respect could possibly have agreed to its (treaty) renewal." [5] He also declared that the attitude of the United States stood as the major obstacle to the development of trade.[6] The whole of the sorry demonstration, said the editor, was the work of organized labor and the Pacific Coast states.[7]

When the first news of the threatened boycott reached the New York editor's office, he cited the abuses suffered by the Chinese and urged that the way to solve the problem "is to make it plain that the position of the Government of the United States on this subject is that which the interests of its commerce requires, and not that which is dictated by the prejudice of a clique of labor agitators." [8] In the months ahead, the editor criticized the Commissioner General of Immigration and the Secretary of Commerce and Labor and likewise attacked Theodore Roosevelt for his failure to take a forthright stand. The *Journal of Commerce* observed that its policy accorded with the wishes of the American Asiatic Association and the men of commerce.[9]

Although sympathetic with the Chinese on the issue of immigration, the editor did not entertain the easy assumptions held by some who were friendly to China—that she was about to emerge as a modern and democratic nation taking her place in the family of nations as a friendly partner. No editorial ever expressed the hope that China would become Christian or democratic. The editor, distrustful of the progressive movement and critical of Roosevelt for his assault on the malpractices of business, applied himself to matter-of-fact assessments of developments in China. Mass education and popular suffrage did not necessarily lead to Utopia at home and there was no reason to believe they would in China.

However, the *Journal of Commerce* welcomed prospects of modernization. Japan's victory over Russia, wrote the editor, marked an end to the threat of dismemberment of China and she could now be expected to accept "liberal and progressive ideas." The Chinese, he assured his readers, looked forward to a new era of internal development. A modernized China, able to maintain order, promote stability, and seeing the advantages of opening the interior to trade would bring about a tremendous expansion of American commerce.[10]

The *Journal* opened its columns to Americans residing in China who sought to interpret developments. Bishop Bashford of the Methodists saw the crowding of missionary schools and hospitals as evidence of a friendly feeling toward foreigners.[11] However, Gilbert Reid, President of the American Association in China, did not share Bashford's optimism. Reid wrote: "Beyond the usual antipathy to foreigners there has grown up a party of progressives, who seek to restrict or annul the power and privileges of foreigners acquired under the treaties, and whose patriotic demands and appeals may easily arouse and inflame the more ignorant classes, thus leading to riots." The revolutionary elements "would be only too glad to embroil China with foreign powers." Foreigners in the interior were not as safe as before the Boxer Revolt. The foreigner in the coastal cities was free from danger but only because of foreign-controlled police and the presence of gunboats. Reid, unlike most Americans, concluded: "It is for this reason that, though ideas of popular sovereignty may at first glance stir our enthusiasm, we regard it as far safer for all the Governments to give support to the existing Chinese Government than to give countenance to any party or movement distinct from, or antagonistic to, the Government that is." [12]

The *Journal* did not at first share Reid's fears. In May, 1906, while declaring that China must abide by treaty obligations, the editor commented wryly: "The nervousness manifested in Europe over every new indication of a resolve on the part of China to manage her affairs in her own way is in serious contrast with the general indifference which was shown to the continuous progress of foreign aggression on Chinese territory, and to the obvious determination of some of the great powers to deprive China of the attributes of sovereignty." [13] By April, 1908, the paper was less certain as to the outcome of the developments. It observed "that the impulses which govern the new China are but very partially of our making." Still, this note of philosophical tranquility did not blot out concern. "Curiously enough," said the editor, "this movement to seek instruction from the foreigner is accompanied by a still stronger movement to free China from foreign influence." He accepted the fact that there was "an unalterable determination among all intelligent Chinamen to have done, once and for all, with foreign dictation in the internal affairs of their country. . . ." [14] By May, 1910, the *Journal* considered Chinese hostility probably "the most pressing aspect of the Far Eastern question."

Although the close attention paid to China suggests that the *Journal of Commerce* viewed her as of primary importance, cautious analysis of the editorial policy makes it clear that this was not so. The editor began with the assumption that the fantastic development of the economy of the United States required foreign markets. These were to be found in Europe, the Middle East, Africa, Asia, and South America. China fitted into this larger pattern. The first editorial for 1907 outlined the major national and international problems "of such unusual gravity that thoughtful men stand mute in their presence." These problems, he saw, as fourfold:

> the unendurable abuses of the power and privileges of corporate institutions . . . ; the serious tendency towards the displacement of British democracy by a rampant socialism; the rapid consolidation of socialistic institutions on the Continent, and especially in Germany; the rapid concentration of political forces in Japan and China; and, . . . , the attitude of Germany as a commercial competitor and an aspirant for the political mastery of Europe.[15]

An occasional editorial implied that China was the alpha and omega in foreign relations, but the editor thought of the Pacific area as a whole and not China alone. Historically, it was the Pacific region that had concerned the United States. The United States had purchased Alaska, acquired Hawaii and the Philippines, and was engaged in building the Panama Canal. These measures were prompted by "our interests as custodians of the gateway to the Pacific." It had been "tacitly assumed," the readers were informed, "that it was virtually essential to our future greatness and prosperity that we should occupy a place of preponderant authority and influence in the great Pacific area in and around which is massed half of the human race." The United States could ill afford any check to its influence on the eastern shores of the Pacific. To permit it would be to "dwarf the role which this republic is fitted to play on the stage of history. . . ." [16] China, as a major part of the Pacific area, was therefore important.

The security of the Pacific Coast and the need for trade determined that Americans should be interested in China. In the early years, the *Journal* shared the general optimism about the potential market in China. Every gain in this trade was carefully noted, but after 1906, these gains allowed little room for exultation and the old optimism disappeared. In 1909, a news article reported that the total value of cotton goods imported by the Orient was four hundred million dollars, but American goods made up only one percent of this total.[17] Another report stated that the U.S. exports to China in 1909 had declined twenty-one percent from the preceding year.[18]

Explanations for the decline were easily come by. Immediately after the war, the piling of huge stocks of cottons in the treaty ports in 1904 sufficed to account for the lull. From 1907 to 1910, the blame was placed on the lack of a stable Chinese currency.[19] In January, 1909, the editor commented on the violent changes in the value of the tael during the past year.[20] He attributed the instability to provincial authorities who emitted or withdrew currency as their own narrow interests prompted. One result was a doubling of the price of rice in the last decade. The fluctuations undermined China's credit and greatly hampered trade due to the increased risks it imposed on merchants.

American businessmen in China, and particularly Consuls stationed in Manchuria, usually blamed Japan but the editor of the *Journal of Commerce* did not become a party to this explanation of his countrymen's failure. He freely admitted that Japan took full advantage of her position in Manchuria but saw in this no grounds for censure.[21]

By 1910, as the visions of a great trade with China faded, the editor probed more deeply into the causes of failure. He was much impressed by the explanation given by Howard Ayres of the China and Japan Trading Company in an address before the National Association of Cotton Manufacturers. Ayres dismissed the explanations of American Consuls in China. The heart of the difficulty, he said, lay in the fact that the United States was not an exporting country. Half of American exports consisted of foodstuffs and raw cotton. In these the United States enjoyed a natural advantage. Ayres noted that "other large figures in a few items make up the greater part of the other half." Other items were exported in only trivial amounts. He concluded, and the editor of the *Journal* agreed, that "so long as we have a great market at home, a fiscal system compelling high prices, and a complacent people so prosperous that they do not care what they pay for what they want, our export trade will not greatly change in character." [22]

When Secretary of State Elihu Root attributed the failures to the American businessmen's predominant concern with the home market, he said, in simplified terms, what Ayres had said.[23] The high tariff policy of the United States and the American currency system hindered exports except where the producer enjoyed natural advantages or where, as in the case of steel, American technology made it possible to produce at a competitive world price.

Others put the blame on lack of American investments. Not until the spring of 1909 did any editorial in the *Journal of Commerce* take up this argument. The editor recognized that loans for railway construction were usually accompanied by agreements that the equipment be purchased in the country of the bankers making the loan. However, the immediate stimulus for arguing in favor of investment came from the sharp decline in interest rates and the abundance of "cheap money" early in 1909. The *Journal of Commerce* was disturbed by this development and especially worried about its leading to excessive speculation in the stock market. In March, in a long editorial on railway loans to China, it stated:

The failure of American capital to be represented in these issues must be held to be matter for regret, since, even in the absence of any explicit bargain to that effect, the purchase of rails and equipment is very likely to be made in the country which furnishes the money. . . . On the general basis of five percent money, there need be no difficulty in placing American capital in large amounts in China, preferably in combination with other international lenders in the same field. In the existing condition of the domestic demand for the finished products of iron and steel, some large orders from China would furnish highly seasonable and welcome relief.[24]

When the Department of State, led by Willard Straight, promoted a consortium of New York banks and demanded that they be granted a share in the loans for the construction of the Hukuang railways in Central China, the editor was jubilant. The bankers, he said, are today the arbiters of peace and war, "thus America does well to win a place for herself in the Orient so influential that she may not only find profitable employment for capital, but may be a power for the preservation of equitable peace in that part of the world." [25] American participation would likewise, he noted, enhance the chances of increasing the share of American business of China's trade.

Missionaries and scholars who sought to understand China were interested in China for reasons quite different than those that motivated a sector of the business community. They did not concern themselves with the possible importance of China to the United States; their interest was in China itself, her present condition and the changes that were gaining momentum. These changes had their approval. They applauded the abolition of the classical civil service examinations in 1905, the establishment of new schools, the construction of railroads, and the launching of a series of political reforms. Each and every move toward modernization received acclaim. The *Missionary Review of the World* reported:

> A people counting one in four of the world's population; an immense territory of unlimited resources; national characteristics of an extraordinary type—sobriety, patience, industry, cheerfulness, resourcefulness; a national feeling powerful, tho in the past unorganized. Childish superstitions, crude arts and a cramping educational system have dwarfed its life. But their spell is broken.[26]

The writer, a missionary, listed the changes taking place. Another hailed the waking up and called for patience and understanding should the transformation be accompanied by violence against the foreigner—"She has occasion to hate Western nations, and if her vengeance is stirred, it is not strange." [27] Before the changes have run their course, wrote one missionary, every European and every American will be banned from his position and the door closed to Christianity, but he could not but share to some degree the enthusiasm of the young and old as their voices cried out: "A new day! A new day." [28] The Reverend H. G. C. Hollock, writing from Shanghai, said that the leaders of China now saw that the hope lay "in widespread education, better civilization, more improvements, better laws, purer rulers, a change in the methods of government, and a living religion." The Chinese, seeing that these were all-important, were "throwing themselves heart and soul into a quest for them." [29] At the Student Volunteer Convention in 1906, Robert R. Gailey, another missionary, told his listeners that he was not going to discuss China's conservatism, superstition, ignorance, nor the uncivilized customs, such as footbinding. "Not of these things, out of which has grown the impression that China is uncivilized, shall I speak, but I am going to talk for a moment of a new China,...." [30]

No missionary enjoyed a wider audience than Arthur H. Smith whose books on China were known for their wealth of information and sprightly style. In 1906, he returned to the United States on furlough. During his five and a half months at home, Smith delivered one hundred and seventy lectures.[31] In 1907, his book, *China and America To-Day*, came off the press. At a time when few Westerners grasped the depth of the humiliation that China had suffered, Smith warned that the new China would no longer tolerate interference and exploitation. He stated the case for the Chinese:

> Your legalized opium has been a curse in every Province into which it penetrated, ... Your people are everywhere extra-territorialized; but instead of a grateful return for this ill-advised stipulation, they appear to act as if there were no laws in China, and this encourages native lawlessness and makes constant difficulties for every native official. ... Your newspapers vilify our officials and our government.... What countries give aliens the extraterritorial status? What countries allow aliens to compete in their coasting

trade? What countries throw open their inland waters to other flags? And yet all these things you compel us to grant you! Why can you not treat us as you treat others?[32]

Smith declared that the West could no longer treat China in this manner. "It is imperative that there should be a radical readjustment of the relations between the West and the East."[33]

Smith described the achievements of the new China: the beginnings of a modern army, railroads, the increased use of steam-driven ships, an improved postal system, vocational schools, and the establishment of modern industry. He admired the sons of Han because they would assert themselves and "manage their own affairs—as they are abundantly competent to do."[34] "On account of the lack of capital, of competent Chinese engineers, and of experienced (not to say honest) administrators, no confidence is yet felt by foreigners in China in the practicability of developing China on these lines," he observed, and then laid bare for all to see a fact the West was not yet ready to accept: "under present conditions, China must either be developed thus or remain undeveloped, for foreign domination or interference the Chinese will no longer tolerate. Their evident wish and intention is to buy out as speedily as possible all foreign 'rights' and thus make an end of them."[35]

One of the best known missionaries, W. A. P. Martin, formerly President of the Imperial University in Peking, in 1907, hailed the new era in his book *The Awakening of China*. In the previous four years, declared Martin, "more sweeping reforms have been decreed in China than were ever enacted in a half-century by any other country, if one excepts Japan, whose example the Chinese profess to follow, and France, in the Revolution of which Macaulay remarks that 'they changed everything from the rites of religion to the fashion of a shoe-buckle.' "[36] John R. Mott, leader of the missionary movement on the home front, welcomed the changes taking place although he feared that agnosticism and materialism would triumph unless the western churches supported missionary work with greater earnestness.[37] Courtenay Hughes Fenn, a Presbyterian missionary stationed in Peking, described the changes in an article entitled "China's Divine Discontent." China, now awakened to her needs and what she could learn from the West, inspired sympathy and hope.[38]

These spokesmen, who had dedicated their careers to China, never doubted her future importance. From their point of view, the United States could not afford to ignore China, and their own humanitarian concerns made them imperialists of righteousness.

Scholars, like missionaries, succumbed to the enchantment of the Celestial Empire. Professor Jeremiah Jenks of Cornell University, who had formerly served as a consultant to the Chinese Government, pleaded for understanding. He contended that Americans had misjudged the Chinese because "their ideals are different from ours, thinking them backward when they are merely different; uncultural, simply because they do not care for our culture; degraded because some of their practices, being strange to us, have seemed to us wrong." [39] The great virtues in China's civilization were usually overlooked. Jenks thought that "nowhere else in the world, perhaps, is there today so active and so universal a regard for the higher learning, as they understand it, so universal and profound a reverence for the teachers of culture and morals,. . . ." Now China was changing, "and in our direction."[40] He cited the beginnings made in transportation, the establishment of schools, the appointment of younger men to administrative positions, and the efforts to centralize the Government.

A well-known professor of sociology, Edward Alsworth Ross, after studying the Chinese and their society at first hand, presented his findings in *The Changing Chinese*. Ross saw great potential being released as individuals became emancipated from reverence for the past, a reverence understandable because their ways had served them so admirably. Once reverence for the past was dissipated by curiosity about the present and future, these intelligent, industrious and stable people would make rapid strides. This was already happening.

Ross informed his countrymen that practically all foreigners "who are capable of sympathy with another race become warm friends of the Chinese." It was "the solid human qualities of the folk" that appealed. "The fact is," wrote Ross, "the Chinese are extremely likable and those who have known them longest like them best." [41]

The professor acknowledged that the problems standing between China as she was and as she could become were staggering. Overpopulation created a frightening tension between agricultural production and sheer subsistence.[42] The value system, with its premium on numerous progeny, perpetuated the problem.[43] The lowly position of women in Chinese society prevented them from having full influence on their children.[44] The general practice of nepotism and the desire for quick reward stood in the way of the development of industry.[45] The general attitude that manual labor constituted a mark of inferiority was another problem.[46] The way the Chinese insisted on clinging to traditional studies and allowing little time for practical learning impeded the preparation of young people for the new society.[47] Putting one's individual interests above all others plagued the management of every enterprise and the same attitude helped explain the wide-spread practice of pilfering. Ross reported that the Peking-Hankow Railway complained "of the nightly theft of ringbolts and plates; no fewer than 60,000 bolts a month and 10,000 plates per annum. . . ."[48]

These practices had their source in the social order with its limited intellectual horizons and constant struggle for sheer subsistence. The reader did not love the Chinese less but rather more as Ross portrayed them as victims of archaic social arrangements. How to help these industrious, good-natured, and able people achieve what they so richly deserved emerged as the major point. Therefore, he could close his book with this heroic peroration.

The Crucifixion was two hundred and eighty years old before Christianity won toleration in the Roman Empire. It was one hundred and twenty-eight years after Luther's defiance before the permanence of the Protestant Reformation was assured. After the discovery of the New World one hundred and fifteen years elapsed before the first English colony was planted here. No one who saw the beginning of these great, slow, historic movements could grasp their full import or witness their culmination. But nowadays world processes are telescoped and history is made at aviation speed. The exciting part of the transformation of China will take place in our time. In forty years there will be telephones and moving picture shows and appendicitis and sanitation and baseball nines and bachelor maids in every one of the thirteen hundred *hsien* districts of the Empire. The renaissance of a quarter of the human family is occurring before our eyes and we have only to sit in the parquet and watch the stage.[49]

How could anyone fail to see that China was the great question of the Twentieth Century? Here was the center of human drama, full enough of misery to soften the hardest heart, rich enough in human potential to carry aloft the most prosaic minds on wings of imagination. Markets, balance of power, security, cold calculations of national interest paled before this vision. The American people had fought, worked, and kicked over the traces of older societies and made dreams come true. How could they be indifferent when China with a large portion of the human race cut its ties with the dead past and embarked on another experiment that would liberate men's minds and energies for the building of a new society?

No large segment of the American public took China as seriously as those very vocal and enthusiastic missionaries and scholars. That their image of China was not generally shared is made clear by an analysis of two magazines that catered to the educated and reasonably well-informed, namely, the *Review of Reviews* edited by Albert Shaw and the *Outlook* edited by Lyman Abbott.

The *Review of Reviews* prided itself on informing Americans about developments around the world. However, the apathy and superficiality of its treatment of China may be seen in the limited coverage given to the question and in the nature of its editorial comments. Editorials dealing with China never challenged the idealistic picture of the majority of the missionaries and invariably assumed that China policy was guided by good wishes for China. When matched against the outpourings of an A. H. Smith, W. A. P. Martin, or E. A. Ross, those editorials had no more passion than a weather report.

The journal divided itself into three major parts: The Progress of the World, Articles, and Leading Articles of the Month. The first of these sections, more than one-third of each issue, was made up of the editor's report and comments upon happenings at home and abroad. Albert Shaw wrote this entire section himself.

Analysis of this section for the year 1907 shows that two hundred and forty-six column inches were devoted to the domestic railroad question, one hundred and fifteen to Great Britain, eighty-four to Germany, one hundred and seventy-three to France, one hundred and fifteen to Japanese immigration, seventy-seven to Japan itself, and eighteen to China. Of course, newsworthy events dictated allotment of space in part and so there were shifts from year to year in the portion given to each country or question. This is reflected in the allotments of column space in 1911 when revolutionary disturbances in China gained her greater attention. In that year, the railroad question in American politics gave way to discussion of other domestic issues; consequently, it now occupied only sixty column inches. Domestic happenings in France and Germany, now less dramatic than earlier, received thirty-five and thirty-two inches respectively. However, international diplomacy replaced European domestic affairs and in consequence Europe continued to serve as the focus of attention. Moreover, developments in Great Britain now crowded in to the extent of one hundred and seventy-nine column inches. China, thanks to the outbreak of the revolution in October, occupied seventy-nine inches.

In each issue the *Review of Reviews* ran five or six articles. Not until 1911 was there an article on China and then there were three late in the year. This paucity of attention to China was not a product of the nature of the magazine or any peculiar lack of interest in China on the part of the editor. As a matter of fact, the *Review of Reviews* gave more attention to China than almost any other periodical.

Albert Shaw believed that the only interest of the United States in China lay in trade. In February, 1905, in the course of the Russo-Japanese War, he defended Hay's policy of seeking the neutralization of China and the strongly pro-Japanese sympathies of Americans. "By the way," wrote Shaw, "if those Russians who cannot understand why American sympathies, which follow American interests, should go to Japan in the war will study the figures of last year's American trade with Manchuria, they will find in the figures . . . an answer conclusive, if not satisfactory." [50] The editor never examined in any of his writings the basic question of what interests the United States did have in China. He simply asserted that she had an interest in China's markets. Perfunctory observations on the importance of trade in reporting developments in Manchuria continued to characterize Shaw's editorials from 1905 through 1910. The offhand character of these observations suggest that reference to trade, when discussing China, had become a habit. There was never any careful analysis of the trade nor any thoughtful reflection on the question of its importance.

The major note struck by Shaw in his brief reports was China's progress. "Even China Moves" told of the plan for a constitution and observed: "It is becoming increasingly evident that the basis of all the ferment in the Chinese Empire during the past few years has been a general desire to advance along the lines of Western civilization." [51] Other editorials recorded the campaign against opium, the meetings of the Provincial Assemblies, the promise of a parliament, the opening of schools, and the building of railroads. These editorials, little more than scanty references that gave a few bare facts, hailed the progress of the Chinese.

The friendly observations on China were never accompanied by a discussion of the deeper conflicts, the great obstacles to change, or the quite superficial nature of the indices employed in estimating the degree of change. They differed sharply from the writings of the missionaries and other friends of China in their lack of commitment to the view that China was of major importance.

In the *Outlook,* another periodical of major standing in the years prior to the First World War, the same editorial policy of casual and measured friendliness to China prevailed. Likewise, the *Outlook* commented briefly but with regularity on China's progress. The interests of the United States, wrote the editor, were commercial. "Throughout the world Americans are acquiring individual and corporate commercial rights." The welfare of the nation was "proportionately dependent on foreign markets. Of them, those of the Pacific bid fair to form the center of the world's commerce and wealth as of its population and power." To promote this commerce, the United States and China should be brought together "commercially, politically, socially, educationally, religiously." He then concluded: "Hence, Chris-

tianity, Protestant Christianity, American Christianity, is the
most effective instrument in bringing together China and America." [52]

China did not seem of sufficient importance to warrant more
than a very occasional reference. From February, 1908, to July,
1909, no editorial mentioned China's importance, but then the
editor suddenly discovered that Russia sought to control the
Municipal Government of Harbin in the railroad zone of the
Chinese Eastern Railway. This inspired another vigorous pronouncement. The editor affirmed: "The time is now past when
Americans could say, 'What do we care for abroad?'" "We
have interests in China, commercial, social, educational, religious," and then he observed: "Interests bring responsibilities." [53]

These responsibilities came to the fore in the *Outlook* whenever Russia appeared aggressive. An editorial in October, 1910,
said there was no danger of war between the United States and
Japan. It was Russia that posed the threat in Asia:

> The most serious menace is Russia. No one who understands that
> Empire believes for a moment that it will permanently accept the
> results of the late war with Japan. All the reasons which led to it
> exist in undiminished force and are intensified by the rage of chagrin and defeat. The factor which now compels peace is the Anglo-
> Japanese Alliance. [54]

However vehemently the *Outlook* expressed itself, its more customary silence on Chinese issues betrayed its protestations and
showed that, at most, it had only a sporadic concern.

The lack of vigilance contrasted sharply with the *Outlook*'s
conviction that the United States had been and was China's
savior. John Hay, time and again, received credit for having
saved China. An editorial entitled "John Hay's Policy Triumphant," informed readers that the Boxer Revolt had "left China
prostrate before designing foes, ready to partition the Empire
geographically, to dismember it politically, to impose upon it
drastic commercial and financial tribute." While the Peking
Government was in exile, Mr. Hay, alone of foreign secretaries,
persisted in treating it as if it did exist and were still worthy of
respect. The Chinese responded to this highminded and far
seeing course. "The result was that Mr. Hay saved the Empire's
geographical, political, and commercial integrity. He did more,

he preserved the Chinese Government from the imposition upon it of a rapacious indemnity for alleged losses by the Powers during the rebellion and in payment for their services in ending it." [55]

Again, in July, 1909, the editor of the *Outlook* repeated the exact wording of the above editorial and supplemented it with an explanation of Hay's watchdog activity when the Russians attempted to consolidate their control over Manchuria after the Boxer Revolt. The editorial summed it up: "China thus owes more to John Hay than to any other man." [56]

Of course, the editor of the *Outlook* was not alone in his adulation of John Hay and the assistance he had rendered to China. One contributor, Elbert F. Baldwin, after praising John Hay, said: ". . . it ought not to be difficult for us to continue to be the leader of China's friendly advisers." Then he went on to heap praise upon the role of the United States: "Foremost among nations is America in defending 'China for the Chinese.' Have we not saved her land from being partitioned among the Powers? Has not our friendship been manifested since then, especially in times of famine and flood?" [57]

The Hay myth, like other myths, was not necessarily wholly lacking in reality but it conformed more to the apparent need of his generation for assurance that the United States counted for something in world affairs, and the "something" was morality and justice. Eventually, the myth itself became a factor shaping China policy even though more realistic considerations had a preponderant influence.

The images of China varied from one part of the American community to the other. Each was essentially friendly as opposed to hostile, but only a very small group of missionaries and a handful of scholars considered China to be of predominant importance and wished to see the U.S. Government make every effort to defend China. The two major periodicals, the *Review of Reviews* and the *Outlook,* in spite of professing friendship, failed to demonstrate a serious interest. In fact, these two magazines treated China more as a matter of curiosity than as a major problem in the foreign relations of the United States. Other periodicals, if anything, took China even less seriously. The *Journal of Commerce* was a voice in the wilderness.

NOTES

1. "The Chinese Trouble," *The Commercial and Financial Chronicle,*
   May 3, 1906, p. 480.
2. *The Commercial and Financial Chronicle,* June 6, 1908, p. 1367.
3. *Ibid.,* January 15, 1910, p. 137.
4. "The New Responsibilities of China," *The Journal of Commerce and
   Commercial Bulletin,* September, 1905, p. 4.
5. "How Not to Promote Commerce," *ibid.,* May 1, 1905, p. 4.
6. *Ibid.*
7. "Commerce and the Chinese Exclusion Laws," *ibid.,* June 12, 1905, p. 4.
8. *Ibid.*
9. "President Acts for the Chinese," *ibid.,* June 26, 1905, p. 1.
10. "Enlarged Markets for Cotton Products," *ibid.,* February 20, 1905, p. 4.
11. "The Real Chinese Danger," *ibid.,* February, 1906, p. 4.
12. "Situation in China no Cause for Alarm," *ibid.,* May 14, 1906, p. 1.
13. "China and the Powers," *ibid.,* May 14, 1906, p. 4.
14. "China in the Council of Nations," *ibid.,* April 6, 1908, p. 4.
15. "The Drifts of 1907," *ibid.,* January 7, 1907, p. 4.
16. "Mastery of the Pacific," *ibid.,* September 30, 1907, p. 4.
17. "U.S. Interest Small in Commercial Orient," *ibid.,* April 12, 1909, p. 9.
18. "China's Imports," *ibid.,* September 12, 1910, p. 8.
19. "Parity of International Exchange in Asia," *ibid.,* January 11, 1909, p. 4.
20. *Ibid.*
21. "The Dominant Interest in the Far East," *ibid.,* January 13, 1908, p. 4.
22. "Common Sense about Exports," *ibid.,* May 2, 1910, p. 4.
23. *Ibid.*
24. "Chinese Railroad Loans," *ibid.,* March 15, 1909, p. 4.
25. "Financial Conditions," *ibid.,* June 14, 1909, p. 3.
26. "Signs of the Times," *The Missionary Review of the World,* April, 1906,
    p. 305.
27. "Apathy of China Broken," *ibid.,* June, 1906, pp. 405–406.
28. Reverend C. Benson Barnett, "China's Outlook from Within," *ibid.,*
    XIX (August, 1906), 583.
29. The Reverend H. G. C. Hollock, "The Day of Opportunity in China,"
    ibid., XIX (September, 1906), 660.
30. *Students and the Modern Missionary Crusade, Addresses Delivered be-*

fore the Fifth International Convention of the Student Volunteer Movement for Foreign Missions, Nashville, Tennessee, February 28–March 4, 1906 (New York: Student Volunteer Movement for Foreign Missions, 1906), p. 335.

31. "Dr. Smith a 'Traveling Bishop,' " *The Missionary Review of the World,* XIX (September, 1906), 706.

32. Arthur H. Smith, *China and America To-Day: A Study of Conditions and Relations* (London: Oliphant, Anderson and Ferrier, 1907), p. 105.

33. *Ibid.,* pp. 106–107.

34. *Ibid.,* p. 129.

35. *Ibid.,* p. 123.

36. W. A. P. Martin, *The Awakening of China* (New York: Doubleday, Page and Co., 1907), p. 199.

37. John R. Mott, *The Decisive Hour of Christian Missions* (New York: Student Volunteer Movement for Foreign Missions, 1911), p. 64.

38. Courtenay Hughes Fenn, "China's Divine Discontent," *The Independent,* LXII (June 27, 1907), 1511.

39. Jeremiah Jenks, "The Progress China is Making," *The Review of Reviews,* XXXI (May, 1905), 595.

40. *Ibid.*

41. Edward Alsworth Ross, *The Changing Chinese: The Conflict of Oriental and Western Cultures in China* (New York: The Century Co., 1911), p. 63.

42. *Ibid.,* pp. 66, 96.

43. *Ibid.,* pp. 96, 101.

44. *Ibid.,* p. 212.

45. *Ibid.,* pp. 125, 127, 134.

46. *Ibid.,* pp. 336–337.

47. *Ibid.,* p. 328.

48. *Ibid.,* p. 83.

49. *Ibid.,* pp. 344–345.

50. "Our Interest and Stake," *The Review of Reviews,* February, 1905, p. 152.

51. "Even China Moves," *ibid.,* October, 1906, p. 411.

52. "China and America," *The Outlook,* February 15, 1908, pp. 374–377.

53. "Russia's Aggressions in China," *ibid.,* July 31, 1909, pp. 773–774.

54. "Will There Be War in the Far East," *ibid.,* October 1, 1910, pp. 258–260.

55. "John Hay's Policy Triumphant," *ibid.,* January 25, 1908, p. 149.

56. "American Relations with China," *ibid.,* July 31, 1909, p. 773.

57. Elbert F. Baldwin, "Mexico and China," *ibid.,* May 24, 1910, pp. 82–85.

CHAPTER VIII

THE FRAMEWORK OF AMERICAN DIPLOMACY
IN CHINA

THE DIPLOMATS, their spirits made tranquil by knowledge and experience, exhibited firmness but not urgency. They had a full understanding as to how the heritage of treaties and agreements circumscribed freedom of diplomacy, and above all a sharp cognizance of the fact that the United States had only a minor economic stake in China and that the interest of the public at large was no more than cursory. W. W. Rockhill wrote to his colleague, J. V. A. MacMurray, in 1913, "Were we, are we or will we ever be—until a radical change has come over us—willing as a country to discharge duties and responsibilities as we would be expected to by the other foreign governments participating with us in these undertakings? I see no sign that we will;. . . ." [1] Diplomats labored loyally for the ideal of the Open Door but always with full knowledge that present interests did not justify an aggressive policy.

The Open Door Policy, especially after 1905, lacked a firm mooring to the realities of Asia. When the danger was a partition of China, the policy had more relevance, but this was no longer the situation. The race for territory and spheres of influence was over. Consequently, all nations willingly professed their adherence to the Open Door. In so doing they proclaimed that while no longer interested in rape, their lust was now directed to more practical matters. Railway contracts, mining rights, and other enterprises rather than territory absorbed their attention. The capitalists of Europe spearheaded the drive and their Governments supported them. This support was restrained only by the political concerns of the home governments. Prospective contracts for enterprises in the political bailiwick of an ally could only be supported at the risk of losing the allied nation's cooperation in the maintenance of more important interests. For instance, London firmly refused to support a British corporation that secured a contract to construct the Fakumen Railway within Japan's sphere in South Manchuria.[2] The British Government, whose primary concern in Asia was the security of India, could not afford to offend her ally. Other governments operated under similar restraints in supporting their business interests. However, politics did not seriously hamper the business classes. Investments in China doubled from 1900 to 1914.[3] The Open Door Policy provided no protection to either Chinese or American interests in this new situation.

If the United States was to take the lead in the Far East, then it, too, would presumably have to lead the way in investments. These were the measure of a nation's influence in China and, equally important, only a large stake in China could justify a strong policy, vigorously implemented, by Washington. The United States sought to compete with large shareholders in the China enterprise while holding almost no shares itself.

The Department of State, compared to the leading Foreign Offices of Europe, stood guard over only minor economic interests. In 1914, British business investments totaled $607.5 million, or 37.7 percent of all foreign investments in China. Russia with $269.3 million, Germany with $263.6 million, Japan with $219.6 million, and France with $171.4 million ranked next in order. American business interests amounted to $49.3 million, but 3.1 percent of the total.[4]

With investments went control over railways, mines, and other enterprises, the very basis of the new economy emerging in China. The British gained an early lead in the railroad field, and the investors invariably demanded guarantees that meant control. The most important of the British railway agreements specified that the chief engineer, the fiscal officer, and the majority of the board of directors should be British. In the early years, these arrangements could be justified on grounds of Chinese lack of experience in managing large transportation systems, but thereby a precedent was set that was adhered to long after the Chinese were competent to run railways themselves.

Foreigners demanded guarantees that went well beyond reasonable assurance of security for their investments. The British and Chinese Corporation, financiers of the railway from Peking to Newchwang, held a first mortgage on both the property and the earnings of the line. This adequate protection of the British investment was further buttressed by a provision that the Imperial Government of China "unconditionally guaranteed and declared itself responsible for the payment of the principal and interest." The loan agreement also stipulated that the chief engineer should be British, and the principal members of the staff European. Consequently, the Chinese, although they owned almost as many shares of stock as the value of the British loan, had no control. In addition to controlling the railway, the British also dominated the car and locomotive works at Tongshan and the Shanhaikwan Works associated with the railway company.[5] These, in turn, manufactured equipment according to British design, thereby giving British manufacturers of similar types of equipment an advantage in selling to other railways in China.

At least technically, business arrangements of this sort did not conflict with the U.S. policy of the Open Door. To have countered this movement Americans would have had to pursue a similar course of eagerly promoting investments. This was precisely what they did not do. The result, as J. Newton Nind, an American trade journalist, wrote after a tour of China, was that Great Britain had come to dominate the Orient.[6] The absence of investment had its counterpart in a lack of any serious interest in the China market on the part of American manufacturers. A writer for the *Far Eastern Review* observed: "With the complete indifference of American manufacturers to this great field, and their refusal to look the situation square in the face, there is only one termination to the unequal contest." Whatever "progress had been made to date with American cars and rolling stock in China," this writer reported, "is largely due to the push and hustle of the Japanese." The sale of American locomotives and railway cars in China was due to the enterprising spirit of the Japanese Mitsui Company and not to the efforts of the American manufacturers.

Speaking before the American Manufacturers' Export Association in September, 1911, William C. Redfield, business executive, member of Congress and the Secretary of Commerce under Woodrow Wilson, explained how manufacturers in England and

Germany were aggressive because these two countries must export or die due to the limitations of their home markets. "Here in America," said Redfield, "the reverse is true." American industries developed "with a proper and sole regard to our domestic needs. Out of this same background, has grown the peculiar outlook of the American manufacturer upon the foreign field. To him it is not or has not been the chief market he seeks, but rather an incidental one." [7] To be sure, Redfield now saw a need for foreign markets and urged their importance, but the whole burden of his address was the lack of interest and failure of American manufacturers to develop markets abroad.

In a situation where influence depended to a considerable degree on investment and commercial ties, the weakness of the United States quite obviously lay in the fact that its China policy had no substantial economic undergirding. With no economic roots in China sufficient to nourish a strong will the United States found it difficult to rise above the rank of an onlooker.

The absence of American economic enterprise had its parallel in the absence of pressing security considerations. Admittedly, Theodore Roosevelt became restive and saw in the Philippines the American Achilles' heel. Men like Thomas F. Millard, Frederick McCormick and some other journalists, including the editorial writer for the New York *Journal of Commerce,* on occasion stressed that the United States had an interest in permanent peace in the Far East but they did not suggest that there was any cause for alarm. Nor does the evidence demonstrate that pleas of friendship and cooperation with Japan were motivated by fear of that country. Nor is there any suggestion in diplomatic correspondence of any pressing concern that the security of the United States or her possessions was threatened. However, it is true that the General Board of the Navy Department was sufficiently concerned to draft plans for the conduct of a war with Japan. [8] This meant that they accepted such a war as a possibility, not that they counted on it as a probability.

It was quite otherwise with the other major Pacific Powers. Japan lived in fear of another Russian campaign and Russia clearly feared Japan. Great Britain worried about India and her close working relations with Japan reflected her need for an ally to counter possible Russian aggressiveness. France, in turn, with her important holdings in Southeast Asia, her heavy investments in Russia, and fear of Germany subordinated her China policy to these considerations. By 1911, all of these Powers were tied together in agreements and alliances and each was thereby free, within some generally accepted limitations, to push its own interests in its respective spheres. Their linkage in China offered a bulwark against the United States effectively challenging any one of them, a fact noted more than once by contemporary observers.

The diplomacy of the United States inevitably reflected the weakness of both economic and security considerations. Public sentiment on the China question never rose to peremptory demands simply because neither special interest groups nor broad national security interests so dictated. Little more was required of the Department of State than to show occasional reverence for the widely acclaimed Hay policy, to affirm the principle of equality of commercial opportunity, and publicly to approve the missionary enterprise. Of course, the China question would have quickly blazed into the headlines if the Philippines had been attacked or Americans in China fallen victim to assault. In the absence of these contingencies even Theodore Roosevelt was tamed into the mood of the psalmist when he would have preferred playing the role of Joshua.

The years prior to the Russo-Japanese War permitted occasional trumpeting of righteousness in the wake of the Anglo-Japanese Alliance, but in the aftermath of the war, the whole power structure in Asia was so altered as to place a premium on unimpassioned watchfulness. At a dinner given by the Asiatic Institute in New York on November 12, 1914, W. W. Rockhill said: "we fought manfully for five years for the maintenance of the open door in every corner of the Chinese Empire, even though in so doing we may have temporarily strained the good relations we always wish to maintain with the whole world."[9] Since then, leadership had passed to Japan. Granted that Rockhill, as a major figure in dealing with Chinese affairs in the earlier period, was not free of bias, the fact remains that the U.S. role diminished.

Three factors explain the decline. Prior to 1905, a natural affinity with Japan and Great Britain in opposition to Russia made it easier and less hazardous to assert the American policy without danger of entrapment in an exposed diplomatic position. Second, Japan's amazing success in following up the gains she made at Portsmouth with an economic and commercial effort which was largely at the expense of the commerce of the United States made the close cooperation with her in the earlier period more difficult. Finally, the China problem itself changed in two respects. The partition by the major Powers was no longer a danger to China, but a more subtle and less direct control by means of investment in railroad and mining enterprises. This was accompanied by a failure of American investment to keep pace with the heavy investments by other nationals. Consequently, while the myth of the China market faded, no myth of China as a future place for investment took its place. The Department of State could only carry out a strong policy if influential segments of the public believed that vital interests were at stake.

The period after the Treaty of Portsmouth found those who were important in influencing policy divided into two groups. The old school of diplomats remained sympathetic and cordial to Japan even though concerned about the outcome of Tokyo's obvious energy in establishing her position on the mainland of Asia. The second group, led by Willard Straight, was for the most part younger, in all cases of a less patient temperament and assertive to the point of venturing out into the whirlpool of international politics where they might encounter challenges the nation was not prepared to face. They were the predecessors of a generation then being born who would shoulder responsibilities in the far corners of the globe in the name of peace and an orderly world.

In 1905, these two groups, although not rival contestants and while working side by side under a Republican president, parted ways in their approach. Secretary of State Elihu Root, Alvey Adee, the veteran Assistant Secretary, and W. W. Rockhill, who had, behind the scenes, formulated and implemented the policy of John Hay in large part, had long experience in diplomacy.

It was this group that remained in control under the Administration of Theodore Roosevelt. China policy, or the Hay policy, as it was usually called, was not a broadside offensive either in behalf of China or special interest groups at home. The policy had limited aims, namely, an independent China capable of maintaining its position and the development of economic relations mutually advantageous to the American and the Chinese. The Hay program as they professed it aimed at a strong government in China. However, the conditions in Peking sobered their expectations of the Celestial Empire.

In 1905, the officials seemed to have little realization of what was in the Chinese national interest, lacked the ability to bring the ambitions of the provinces and their jealousies of Peking into some reasonable degree of harmony with national interests, and too often the officials were simply incompetent. But it was not only the weakness of Chinese administration that stood in the way of developing a strong China. Few Americans understood as well as did Rockhill the stupendous problems in transforming a Confucian society. The problem was more than political. Rockhill touched upon the central difficulty when he said that the West sought to introduce ideals and materialism; the former the Chinese found inferior to their own and the latter they considered a threat to their national existence.[10] Yet to the devotees of the Hay policy, China would sometime in the future be of great importance and the best service that could be rendered by the United States was an orderly transition to the new state. However, the weakness and anachronism of China made her an unreliable partner in diplomacy as the members of the old school had already learned. Consequently, they were not of a mind to embark on risky adventures in the hope of achieving a goal removed in time and at best uncertain of attainment.

These original supporters of the Open Door Policy accepted the treaty system and made their approach fit the treaty structure. The treaties furnished a basic guide to diplomatic operations. They had no hesitation about holding China to the obligations pressed upon her in the treaties. The primary task of the Legation in Peking was to police the system.

This point of view is well illustrated in the response of the United States to two issues that arose in 1906. After the Russo-Japanese War, China was slow to establish customs stations in the two cities in southern Manchuria she had agreed to open

under the terms of the treaty of 1903. While the major motivation for pressing China on this question was the desire to promote American trade in that area, the correspondence of both
Rockhill and Alvey Adee indicates that holding China to the
treaty provision was also a matter of principle.[11] The second issue
that arose concerned the new spirit of hostility on the part of
the Chinese toward both the unequal treaties and the economic
controls foreigners had acquired. Rockhill commented sympa-
thetically on Chinese aspirations to be masters of their own country and he sided with China on the specific issue of the foreigners' demand that they be permitted to reside anyplace within the
cities to be opened in Manchuria. To permit them to live outside
of a concession would, he said, given the fact that they would not
be subject to Chinese law, create among their Chinese neighbors
a lack of respect for law and order.[12] However, even Rockhill,
who understood the Chinese better than most, inveighed in paternalistic tones against any relaxation of the treaty system. He
advised the Secretary of State that "the measures they are seeking
to enforce should be most closely scrutinized by us before acceptance, and many of them strenuously resisted." [13]

Without the treaties, backed up by force, Westerners would
have been driven out, and the United States no less than any
other nation was determined to maintain the treaty structure as
it had been developed. Although the policy of the United States
called for a strong China, it never hesitated in upholding the
treaties that so seriously compromised Chinese sovereignty. Acting Secretary of State Robert Bacon responded in an arrogant
spirit to Rockhill's communication. Bacon wrote:

> The Government of the United States is determined in its opposi-
> tion to the abridgement of rights now enjoyed by foreigners in the
> settlements or concessions already established or to be enjoyed by
> them in settlements or concessions to be hereafter established.[14]

The treaties protected the foreigners in China against the
hostility of their hosts and made it possible for them to carry on
their many enterprises, both economic and religious; treaties
likewise regulated relations between the Governments whose
nationals held so many important stakes in the Empire. Rights
and priorities granted by China to any one nation were guarded

with a proprietary zeal by the recipient nation, but they were also respected by rival Powers.

American diplomats freely subscribed to an acceptance of the treaty status quo and, in turn, sought to have other nations stay within the limits laid down and not violate agreements made or assurances given. The result was that diplomatic actions were invariably based upon a legal interpretation of treaty provisions or promises that had been made. A protest so based offered some hope of restraining the alleged offender. Where no basis for a protest existed in treaties or in assurances given, a diplomatic inquiry or protest was usually withheld.

Failure to take this into account would lead an historian into distorted interpretations. Silence did not mean approval nor did a legal protest signify that the United States was prepared to take further action. Illustration is to be found in the Open Door Notes of 1899. The Notes did not aim at undoing the spheres of interest or influence recently established by negotiation. As a matter of fact, the Notes acknowledged their existence and then sought to arrange a multilateral agreement whereby "rights" within the spheres would not be further extended. On the basis of the assurance given by the nations in reply, qualified as their answers were, the United States for years to come based much of its diplomatic action.

This acceptance of the treaty system as inviolate obviously circumscribed freedom of action. Unwillingness to override the structure characterized the old school while the more aggressive Philander Knox and Willard Straight sought to circumvent it by bold strokes. The prudence with which the former group approached issues in China is best exemplified in the position its members took on the question of presenting the requests of American companies for consideration by the Imperial Government. Shortly after Rockhill arrived at his post, the Legation was asked to transmit to the Chinese Government a letter from A. W. Bash of the China Investment and Construction Company requesting participation in a railway loan. Rockhill declined to do so and wrote to the Secretary of State for further instructions. He explained: "If the legation is in duty bound to do what Mr. Bash requests it to, then in the eyes of the Chinese all his communications would have official support. This I hardly think is what the Department wishes."[15] Rockhill explained to Mr. Bash that while he could not give official support to a request, he would gladly come to the company's defense if it were "deprived of a treaty right or unfairly discriminated against. . . ."

Alvey A. Adee prepared a memorandum for Secretary Root giving his views on Rockhill's position. He thought Rockhill's principle "would hold good in any except Oriental countries." "China," wrote Adee, "like the other Eastern Governments, looks upon any privilege granted to foreign citizens or corporations as a favor to the foreign government. Our position has been the opposite of this, for we expect our agents to be scrupulous in avoiding any appearance of soliciting favors for Americans or American corporations." Adee doubted that this policy had "worked to the disadvantage of our citizens to any great extent, for they have secured a number of concessions in China." His final recommendation was that no harm would be done if applications were forwarded without comment by the Legation to the Chinese Government.[16] The only policy of the United States in this regard was that all reputable American applicants should have the same opportunity to compete as applicants of any other nationality. This conservative position reflected the fact that American business was not really serious about economic opportunities in China.

Against this background and tradition took place the more stirring developments in relations between the United States and China during the Second Administration of Theodore Roosevelt, immediately following the Russo-Japanese War. According to Eugene Dooman, who was serving under Lloyd Griscom in the U.S. Legation in Tokyo, and contrary to the traditional historical account, the initiative in the peacemaking took place there rather than in the White House. It was Griscom, at a soiree given by Baron Komura, Japan's Minister for Foreign Affairs, who informally asked Baron Komura "whether the Japanese Government had formulated its peace terms and was prepared to disclose them." Griscom did so wholly on his own initiative. Komura appeared startled but excused himself and said "that he would communicate shortly with Griscom." Later that evening, Komura led Griscom to a private room and they met briefly with Premier Katsura who explained that Japan "had already fixed upon the terms for ending the war and would disclose them in confidence to a third party if the Russian Government were prepared to disclose its peace terms.[17]

Theodore Roosevelt eagerly seized the opportunity and sounded out Russia forthwith. In September, the representatives of the two warring nations met at Portsmouth, New Hampshire. The negotiations reached an impasse on the two issues of future control of Saghalin and an indemnity. The President urged Japan to forego an indemnity and to settle for half of Saghalin. Japan, it had already been agreed, was to take over all of Russia's rights in southern Manchuria, including the naval base at Port Arthur and the important railway. She sacrificed only a small part of the rich fruits of victory in yielding to Roosevelt but in Tokyo an embittered populace rioted in protest before the American Legation. Japan came out of the war desperately in debt but in a stronger position on the mainland of Asia than Russia had enjoyed before hostilities. Unlike Russia, she had no European frontier to divert her energies and her navy could not be challenged by any one Power in the waters off China. Roosevelt observed the new power alignment with misgiving and asked W. W. Rockhill for his opinion. The new Minister in Peking saw no reason for concern. Japan's influence on China would be beneficial.[18] Yet, he, too, acknowledged that he had no doubts that Japan would follow up the advantages she had won with great energy.

However, Japan occupied little of Washington's attention at the close of the war and for a year thereafter. The immigration policy of excluding Chinese, the malignant growth that kept eating away at the healthy tissue so carefully nurtured by men of goodwill, culminated in a crisis in 1905.

The immigration issue had undermined efforts to establish cordial relations ever since the 1880's. In 1894, China felt compelled to sign a treaty excluding all of her citizens from entry into the United States exempting only merchants, students, travelers, and officials. Under the Geary Act of 1892, it fell upon the individual Chinese to prove that he belonged to one of the exempt classes. Immigration officials enforced the law in a hostile spirit. Although the Chinese arriving at an American port had already been certified by an American Consul in China as eligible for admission, the immigration authorities turned them away with great frequency. The officials demonstrated such rigidity that young Chinese already admitted to colleges and universities were sometimes forced, upon their arrival, to return or go to Canada and wait in the hope that friends could interpose in their behalf.

Those Chinese who had migrated earlier or who eluded the fine net of the immigration bureaucracy encountered frequent mistreatment and on occasion, fell victim to riots. Organized labor viewed them as endangering living standards of working-men and the unions pushed legislation hostile to the Chinese. The feeling against them was not limited to labor groups. It flourished in the Pacific Coast states and occasionally in large cities across the country where there were significant numbers of Chinese.

Not until 1905 did China rise in revolt against the exclusion policy and its brutal implementation. In 1904, she adamantly refused to renew the treaty. In the late spring of the following year, merchants and students in the major cities of China launched a boycott of American goods. If we may look at the Boxer movement as representing the old style antiforeignism, the boycott stands as China's first modern demonstration of na-tional resentment against the West. Students provided the leader-ship and mobilized the boycott. The Chinese, said one of the most respected American Consuls, Fleming D. Cheshire, are "taking up the boycott heart and soul."[19] William Woodville Rockhill upon his arrival in Shanghai, found the city placarded with posters protesting against the ill treatment their countrymen had received. In Peking, the new Minister found his desk laden with petitions.

In Washington, Theodore Roosevelt stood between two con-tending groups. The Pacific Coast states were in no mood to yield to pressure from the Chinese and lived in constant fear of an inundation of coolies should the bars be lifted or should the treaty prohibitions be implemented less harshly. However, Roosevelt knew that surrender to their demands would deeply offend the educated classes and church groups who viewed the current policies and practices as benighted and disgraceful. In the better journals, including the *Journal of Commerce,* editors championed the cause of the Chinese with ardor and conviction. Roosevelt undoubtedly shared their view in considerable part, but he found it necessary to steer a middle course.

Caught between two opposing camps, the President looked to a combination of firmness and reasonableness to bring the Chinese to a settlement. He issued an order on June 24 warning immigration officials that Chinese eligible for admission must be accorded the same treatment as citizens of the most favored nation, and that officials guilty of discourtesy or arbitrary treatment would be dismissed. At the same time, in a speech delivered at Atlanta, Roosevelt lofted the issue into the outer realm of morals. "The greatest of all duties is national self-preservation," he announced, "and the most important step in national self-preservation is to preserve in every way the well-being of the worker."[20] Exclusion of Chinese laborers, he then concluded, was necessary to the well-being of the American worker. Having taken this position, he warned the American Minister in Peking: "I intend to do the Chinese justice and am taking a far stiffer tone with my own people than any President has ever yet taken, ... In return it is absolutely necessary for you to take a stiff tone with the Chinese when they are clearly in the wrong."[21]

Rockhill carefully picked his way between the position set forth by his impetuous chief and the realities in China, keeping his eye on the long-term goal. Giving Roosevelt an account of the forces at work and noting that the boycott was a sign of a much to be desired nationalism, he went on to say: "I am fearful to force on such a weak Government the adoption of measures which would result, in all probability, in showing its weakness, when we want to make it stronger, of lessening its authority when we want to make it effective, so that it can discharge its international duties."[22]

The patience of Rockhill, the losses of Chinese merchants, and the ultimate realization of the officials in Peking that it was not in their interest to encourage the discordant elements in the Empire to believe that they could defy the Dynasty with impunity resulted in action. In mid August, the provincial authorities received orders to stop the boycott. On August 31, an Imperial edict was issued condemning the boycott and declaring that Viceroys and Governors would be held responsible for suppressing it.[23] By October, the movement had ceased to the degree that neither Washington nor American commercial interests had cause to protest.

The irony of the United States, with all of its protestations of goodwill toward China, becoming the first target of Chinese nationalism when other nations pursued much harsher policies in China itself, represents the price of domestic attitudes toward the Chinese immigrant. Chinese students coming to the United States learned how insulting the treatment by both immigration officials and the populace could be, and the resulting resentment felt by them and likewise by merchants, more than counterbalanced the genuinely friendly gestures.[24]

Shortly after the close of the Russo-Japanese War, goodwill suffered additional strains as a result of the negotiations carried on between the Peking Government and the American China Development Company.[25] In 1898, this company secured a contract to build a railway from Canton to Hankow. Shortly afterward, the American owners sold a majority of stock to a syndicate of French and Belgian capitalists. In 1904, another group of Americans repurchased the stock. The company showed only casual interest in construction. In 1905, only twenty-seven miles of track, at a cost of three million dollars, had been completed. By this time, the Chinese were gripped by fear of foreign ownership and control of railways and this movement directed itself to demanding cancellation of the contract of the American China Development Company.

There shortly ensued a series of negotiations that reflected no credit on the participants. The Peking Government, responsive to provincial demands but fearful that the Government of the United States would adamantly oppose cancellation, employed devious methods to avoid dealing with Washington. Instead, the Chinese Minister in Washington entered into direct negotiations with the American China Development Company which was now controlled by J. P. Morgan. A deal was arranged whereby the company sold its rights for $6,750,000.[26]

This highly profitable sale did not come to the attention of President Theodore Roosevelt and Secretary of State Elihu Root until it had been agreed upon. They, like Rockhill, viewed the loss as a severe blow to the United States, and Assistant Secretary of State Alvey Adee wired Rockhill on August 15, 1905. "The President does not see how we can submit to such a blow, especially as the concession was largely obtained through the action of the government. . . ."[27] In Peking, Rockhill interviewed Na-T'ung, Minister for Foreign Affairs, but nothing was accomplished. The cancellation of the contract was completed in August.

The loss injured American prestige in China. The high price exacted by the Americans left ill will among the Chinese in the province that took over the contract and three years later when the United States again entered the contest for railway control in Central China, natives of the concerned provinces cited their earlier experience. Americans interested in China continued to refer to the cancellation as the greatest single loss the United States had suffered in China.

The importance attached to the Canton-Hankow Railway contract reflected a growing conviction that if the United States were to have a voice in China, it must have investments. With investment went trade and influence; without it the Open Door diplomacy was reduced to an anachronism. Consequently, in this period the United States found it difficult to regain the initiative it had taken in 1899. In the summer of 1905, for instance, Germany embarked on an aggressive economic development program in Shantung, thereby arousing a concern of Americans that the door to equality of commercial opportunity was being closed and that Germany was dictating political decisions in that province.

However, by the close of 1906, it became clear that Germany had not closed the door to either trade or investment by other nationals. Consequently, the United States had no basis in earlier treaties and diplomatic assurances for protesting. Yet, Germany was clearly gaining the upper hand in Shantung as she developed both mines and railways, leaving the United States an ineffectual bystander. The American Consul in Shantung sought to explain the diminishing importance of the United States in the province as a product of China's fear of German opposition to awarding of economic concessions to Americans. Rockhill promptly dispelled this illusion. Fear of German opposition, he said, did not "effect (sic) our interests a tittle; we would be no more enterprising in Shantung than we are in other provinces in which we have nothing to fear from any foreign or native opposition." Rockhill went on to state:

> American trade out here is distinctly lacking in enterprise. American capital can be too well employed at home to seek an outlet in China, where it may earn 4½ to 5 percent, often with very considerable risk; and American products can be so well sold, in sufficient and ever-increasing quantities, by our present methods, that our merchants do not appreciate the necessity for adopting a more aggressive policy for securing a larger share of the trade in this country.[28]

Obviously, it was a bit awkward to take the rival nation to the woodshed and administer a diplomatic spanking for doing what American business should be doing but did not care to do.

In the light of later developments, the most important question facing the United States was the future course of Japan in Manchuria. Japan's victories over Russia won acclaim. After all, Japan, as Americans saw it, championed the Open Door and her defeat of Russia was a victory for American principles. Those who held posts in the Foreign Service in large part shared this view, but their admiration did not preclude a curiosity as to what Japan might do once she was in control. Even before the end of the war, on July 15, 1905, Lloyd Griscom, Minister to Japan, wrote to Rockhill reporting that two telegrams had appeared in a Japanese newspaper stating that certain towns in Manchuria would be opened exclusively to Japanese traders. "It struck me that under the guise of military measures they are opening up Manchuria to Japanese trade and giving it a very distinct start there—or advantage which would be very hard for our merchants to overcome later," he wrote. He had asked Baron Komura if the report was true. Komura said that it was, "but that it was purely a military measure and that only a limited and carefully selected number of Japanese merchants would be allowed in to facilitate the work of the military authorities." Griscom then telegraphed Washington, but "it fell on barren soil. . . ."[29] He received no reply. In Washington, there was not at that time a mood for questioning Japan. China was causing trouble on the immigration issue and likewise cancelling the contract for the Canton-Hankow Railway while Russia was demonstrating that she could be difficult. At the close of August, Roosevelt wrote to Rockhill:

However, bad as the Chinese are, no human being, black, yellow or white, could be quite as untruthful, as insincere, as arrogant— in short, as untrustworthy in every way—as the Russians under their present system. I was pro-Japanese before, but after my experience with the peace commissioners I am far stronger pro-Japanese than ever.[30]

Griscom did not cease to maintain a watchful eye and in November he applied to the Japanese Government for permission to open Consulates at Mukden and Dalny. His request was turned down on the ground that Mukden was a military base and while the Government postponed giving him a decision on Dalny, Griscom expected a refusal and for the same reason. He wrote to Rockhill that all of the principal towns in Manchuria under Japanese control were freely open to Japanese merchants. To Griscom, it seemed "entirely unfair and contrary to the principle of the open door that they should continue to exclude foreign merchants now that the war is over." [31]

Griscom's judgment implied that once hostilities ceased, then a normal situation prevailed. This did not accord with the facts for China was not prepared to assume her responsibilities. The war had seriously disturbed the situation and the military of necessity had to fulfill a peacekeeping function. In regard to trade, the South Manchuria Railway was almost devoid of equipment, the Russians having sent most of it north into their own area, and this alone handicapped trade.

The complaints during the spring and early summer of 1906 gave no clear indication as to the direction of Japanese policy. The American Association of China, an organization of merchants, attributed a sharp decline of the cotton goods trade to actions of the Japanese, but both Rockhill and James L. Rodgers, Consul-General at Shanghai, thought the decline was due in large part to an abnormal building up of goods during the war. Yet neither questioned that Japanese merchants enjoyed advantages because of Japan's military presence.[32] While the American Association of China was more inclined to emphasize Japan's role, the action they urged was to pressure China into giving "assurances that no preference shall be given to the commerce of any one nation in any part of Manchuria." If China then pleaded inability to offer such assurance, the Secretary of State should make representations to Japan and Russia.[33]

According to three American merchants in Shanghai, the Japanese were evading the payment of duties on imports of their own merchandise, levying heavy duties on both Chinese and foreign goods, and Japanese traders in the interior were freed from paying local taxes. These charges would have carried more weight had not the four Americans who had made the original investigation in Manchuria attributed the prevailing condition to the disorganization resulting from the war. Moreover, these original surveyors of the scene concluded:

> it is most difficult, if not impossible, to offer any satisfactory evidence to substantiate the theory that the Japanese Gov't., through the instrumentality of either its Military or Civil authorities, is at present purposely interfering with or placing any obstacles in the path of other nations for the industrial exploitation of this important part of the Chinese Empire.[34]

They reported that the Japanese enjoyed two advantages: the presence of a large amount of Japanese currency in the area and the failure of China to assume jurisdiction and to establish a customs station at Dalny.

The complexities surrounding the question of conditions of trade in Manchuria by the summer of 1906, defied any easy assessment of blame and of this fact the Department of State, the American Legation in Peking, and the American Consul at Newchwang were well aware. In seeking the restoration of conditions favorable to trade each of these had to take into account a whole series of facts, and Japan's actions were not at the core of the difficulty. She had not only withdrawn her troops from the major centers in the spring of 1906, but she had joined hands with the United States and Great Britain in demanding open treaty ports and the establishment of customs houses. The position taken by the United States was that Mukden and Antung were opened as treaty ports by the Treaty of 1903. No further action was required on this point but China had an obligation under that treaty to establish customs offices and make arrangements for foreign residents.[35]

Japan took the same position but she had some reservations regarding Dairen and then only because she was anxious to be assured that China would establish customs offices in northern Manchuria to collect duties on goods entering by way of Vladivostok. Thomas Sammons, Consul-General at Newchwang, reported to Rockhill in a letter dated July 12, 1906, that conversations with high Japanese officials led him to believe that the Tokyo policy of the Open Door would speedily become effective, "General Fukushima and Mr. Yamaza, the Chief of the Political Division of the Foreign Office, having succeeded, during the past few days, it is stated, in adjusting said policy to heretofore existing conditions of military occupation." [36] Japanese officials, Sammons reported, opposed the establishment of a Maritime Customs House at Mukden, "claiming, with good reasons, that there is no necessity for its existence." [37] Sammons noted: "The Consul General (Japanese Consul at Mukden), as is the case with other Tokyo Foreign Office agents, insists that Japan must have Anglo-Saxon sympathy and support; that it will have this sympathy and support, it is believed, by following in Manchuria practically an Anglo-Saxon policy etc." [38]

On July 24, the Department cabled Rockhill instructing him to seek Japan's cordial cooperation "in the negotiations now pending for the opening of Antung, Hsien and Mukden." In accordance with these instructions, Rockhill called on the Japanese Minister in Peking. Rockhill reported to Root:

> I found Mr. Hayashi's views in perfect accord with my own and he evidenced the strongest desire to see carried out all the steps necessary to ensure in Mukden, An-tung and throughout Manchuria perfect freedom of international trade under equal favorable conditions for all nationalities.[39]

Hayashi admitted that the purchase of all the land in Antung suitable for a settlement was embarrassing, "but it must be remedied by his Government." [40] Rockhill also reported that the Japanese Minister had suggested that the land held by the Japanese in the vicinity of the railway station in Mukden should be incorporated in the international settlement. He considered this an excellent proposal. To this happy report, Rockhill added "that at the present time the chief import into Dalny and An-tung is American flour...." [41]

In the summer of 1906, then, the difficulties appeared to be due only in a minor way to Japan. There were other obstacles. China dragged her feet in all of the negotiations and not without reason. Caught up in the spirit of the "rights recovery movement," Peking found little to be enthusiastic about in the proposals of either the United States or Japan. The opening of Manchuria would increase her revenue but the economic control of the Three Provinces would in all probability fall into other hands, and Americans while never alluding to the prospect, noted frequently how suspicious the Chinese were of Japan. At this same time, Rockhill had his own complaints about the Chinese. On July 6, 1906, he wrote to his old friend Hippisley: "—the Chinese are absolutely impossible to deal with at present—their heads are so swollen—why the Lord only knows! that I prefer to not attempt even discussing matters with them." [42]

The Chinese sought to protect themselves as best they could. Their first point involved a difference of opinion with the United States and Japan on the technical question as to whether Mukden and Antung became treaty ports by the Treaty of 1903 with the United States or by the unilateral action of China. Sammons in Newchwang discussed the issue at length with the Chinese representatives of Peking. "While these representatives are willing to sign a formal agreement," Sammons reported, "the Viceroy and Governor-General assert that under the Shanghai Treaty, Antung and Mukden are to be considered 'self-opened' ports and said Treaty is not to be considered, on this point, like other Treaties concluded by the powers with China." [43] Adee in Washington and Rockhill in Peking had already insisted on quite the reverse. The cities were to be considered as opened by the treaty and it was China's obligation under the treaty now to establish customs offices and provide for foreign residents. [44] The importance of this issue to the Chinese led Sammons to write: "Chinese officials, in fact, as a rule, hold that view and as the Japanese policy seems to be one of declaring these and other places in Manchuria open regardless of China's contention as to settlements etc., the sentiment prevailing among leading Chinese officials is somewhat similar to what Americans would feel if the Monroe doctrine were ignored and disregarded." [45]

Behind this seemingly legalistic controversy lay the whole issue of the right of the Chinese to be masters of their own house. They sought to determine the conditions of foreign ownership of the land in the cities to be opened. Speculation in the land that would eventually become part of the foreign settlements was already under way and both Japanese and Chinese were engaged. The Chinese Government had a long-term goal in view, namely Chinese control. Sammons understood the situation and portrayed it clearly:

> The more serious side of this procedure, however, would seem to be the fact that China is proceeding with its originally outlined settlement plans and will, eventually, be prepared to offer these lands on its proposed short lease terms, being directly contrary to our Treaty, but entirely in accord with its policy of Chinese 'Self-Opened' ports or trade marts. . . .[46]

They were equally concerned about the assumption of both the United States and Japan that the European dominated Imperial Maritime Customs Service would collect the customs in Manchuria. The Chinese deeply resented the fact that the Director, Sir Robert Hart, had failed to appoint a single Chinese to any of the higher posts. This injury to their pride was abetted by the hopes of a number of Chinese officials in Manchuria that they would be appointed to lucrative posts should the Peking Government collect the customs dues directly, rather than having the Imperial Maritime Customs Service collect them.[47]

The major issue from China's point of view concerned control of the customs and the foreign settlements; the obstacles in the way of her achieving this control reached well beyond the more immediate combined pressure of the United States and Japan for the opening of Manchuria. Rockhill explained the whole complicated business to the Secretary of State. The opening of customs houses in southern Manchuria depended on what course Russia pursued in northern Manchuria. The American Minister in Peking thought Russia probably would not raise "any objection of principle," but that it was most unlikely "that it will do anything to facilitate or expedite the carrying out of this provision, unless a *quid pro quo* is offered." Russia wanted to know what was to take place in the south. She also hoped to gain recognition from China "of the innumerable concessions, particularly mining, which Russian subjects have all over Manchuria, and which China is equally desirous of cancelling or refusing to confirm." China did not propose to furnish Russia the opportunity to ask this price by raising the question of collecting customs in the north.[48] China likewise had reasons for delaying an agreement in southern Manchuria until all Japanese military forces were withdrawn. Japan, in turn, marked time hoping that China would force Russia into an agreement.[49]

Rockhill went on to explain another thread in the problem, the insistence by Japan that she receive one-fifth of the customs collected at Dairen. She based this claim on the precedent set by the agreement reached between Germany and China on December 1, 1905, providing that Germany was to receive one-fifth of the customs collected at Kiaochow. An additional obstacle was Japan's argument that she had acquired in Liaotung all the rights which Russia had previously acquired there by agreements with China. Included was the right of the South Manchuria Railway to collect the duties at Dairen. Rockhill noted that China now insisted "that the Custom House shall be purely Chinese without even a foreign commissioner." [50]

Rockhill reported to the Secretary of State that in his conversation with Hayashi, he had expressed the view that while no question could be raised about Japan's legal rights in Dairen, "it would prove most unfortunate if Japan insisted on exercising them." Public opinion abroad, he told Hayashi, would be deeply suspicious as to how Japan exercised her authority.[51]

To break this deadlock, the United States sought to have China stop the collection of duties at Newchwang, the main port of entry for American goods in Manchuria. Hayashi had first suggested this move. The resulting loss of revenue to China, it was thought, would cause her to establish customs offices elsewhere and come to terms on the question of foreign settlements. Rockhill presented it to China as "made chiefly in the interest of China." "If this measure was adopted, both Japan and Russia would urge the prompt establishment of Chinese Customs; . . . ," he argued.[52] However, T'ang Shao-i of the Chinese Foreign Office promptly responded that the duties collected at Newchwang were pledged to the Powers for the Boxer indemnity and it would require the consent of each of them to stop collection.[53]

Early in September, China did declare several cities in Manchuria open to trade, but this was only a formality that had no meaning until arrangements were made for the collection of duties.

China entered into long and difficult negotiations with both Russia and Japan in the autumn of 1906. Both the United States and Great Britain urged on the two Governments the importance of coming to a settlement. In the closing months of these negotiations, the major obstacle to a settlement with Russia was her claim to free entry of goods in a zone one hundred *li* on either side of the border.[54] Russia based this claim on a former treaty and the other Powers did not question the right. In the case of Japan, a most difficult obstacle to settlement was her failure to surrender claims to large amounts of land taken by the military during the war.[55] Another difficulty stemmed from the fact that Japanese had purchased most of the land on the waterfront in Antung leaving no place to locate a customs office. Not until July, 1907, had China come to a settlement with the two Powers who possessed the largest stakes in Manchuria.

Rockhill, as late as October, 1906, advised Root that the decline in American trade in Manchuria was due to other causes than Japanese discrimination. He set forth the opinion that foreigners interested in Manchurian trade "will be offered every opportunity, I may even say inducement, to take a full share in it. The Japanese have not the necessary capital to develop either Manchuria or Korea; foreign capital and enterprise are essential to them to insure the success of enterprises they already have there—such as the South Manchuria Railway—and to repel foreign assistance or put foreign capital under any disadvantage would be simply suicidal." In closing he reminded Root that American merchants did not establish direct relations with their customers, "instead, they depend on Chinese and Japanese—this practice discriminates more against us than any other cause, be it Japanese or Chinese." [56]

In January, 1908, Roger S. Greene, the U.S. Consul in Dairen, wrote a detailed report for the Assistant Secretary of State on commercial conditions. Greene concluded "that in general there is here equal opportunity for all." He admitted that there might be some abuses but he also added "that there is no proof of them to be found." He criticized those who made sweeping and unjust charges, thereby "helping to create a spirit of antagonism that may do immense harm." [57]

NOTES

1. W. W. Rockhill to J. V. A. MacMurray, April 11, 1913, Rockhill Papers, Harvard University Library.
2. Editor, "The Fakumen Railway," *The Far Eastern Review*, VI (November, 1909), 228–229.
3. C. F. Remer, *Foreign Investments in China* (New York: The Macmillan Co., 1933), p. 58.
4. *Ibid.*, p. 76.
5. George Bronson Rea, "Railway Loan Agreements and Their Relation to the Open Door: A Plea for Fair Play to China," *The Far Eastern Review*, VI (November, 1909), 214, 217.
6. G. Newton Nind, "A Study of Trade Conditions in the Orient," *The Far Eastern Review*, VI (July, 1910), 40, 51.
7. "Imperial Railways of North China," *The Far Eastern Review*, November, 1909, p. 234.
8. William C. Redfield, "America's Export Trade," *The Far Eastern Review*, VIII (March, 1912), 327–329.
9. W. W. Rockhill, *Speech Before Asiatic Institute*, New York, November 12, 1914, Rockhill Papers.
10. W. W. Rockhill, Preface to Baroness von Heyking, *Tschun*, manuscript in Rockhill Papers.
11. Rockhill to Root, July 16, 1906, Enclosure No. 3, Memorandum left at Wai-wu Pu, July 13, 1906, by Rockhill; and Adee to Rockhill, August 29, 1906, Department of State Archives.
12. Rockhill to Root, February 15, 1907, Department of State Archives.
13. Rockhill to Root, December 18, 1906, cited by Robert Bacon in Bacon to Rockhill, February 7, 1907, Department of State Archives.
14. *Ibid.*
15. Rockhill to Secretary of State, August 23, 1905, Department of State Archives.
16. Adee to Root, October 3, 1905, Department of State Archives.
17. Eugene H. Dooman to the Editor of the *New York Times*, March 22, 1958, *New York Times*, March 31, 1958.
18. Rockhill to Roosevelt, July 7, 1905, Rockhill Papers.
19. Fleming Duncan Cheshire to Rockhill, June 23, 1905, Rockhill Papers.
20. Theodore Roosevelt's Speech at Atlanta, Georgia, Alfred Henry Lewis

(ed.), *A Compilation of the Messages and Speeches of Theodore Roosevelt, 1901–1905* (Washington: Bureau of National Literature and Art, 1905), p. 693.

21. Roosevelt to Rockhill, August 22, 1905, Rockhill Papers.
22. Rockhill to Roosevelt, October 30, 1905, Rockhill Papers.
23. Rockhill to Root, September 1, 1905, Department of State Archives.
24. For an interesting but shocking account by one Chinese student, *see* Fu Chi Hao, "My Reception in America," *The Outlook,* LXXXVIII (August 10, 1907), 770–773.
25. William R. Braisted, "The United States and the American China Development Company," *The Far Eastern Quarterly,* XI (November, 1951), 147–165.
26. For details of the negotiations, *see* author's *Open Door Diplomat: The Life of W. W. Rockhill* (Urbana: University of Illinois Press, 1952), pp. 72–76.
27. Adee to Rockhill, August 15, 1905, Department of State Archives.
28. Rockhill to Root, December 29, 1906, Department of State Archives.
29. Lloyd C. Griscom to Rockhill, July 15, 1905, Rockhill Papers.
30. Roosevelt to Rockhill, August 29, 1905, Rockhill Papers.
31. Griscom to Rockhill, November 6, 1905, Rockhill Papers.
32. Rodgers to Rockhill, July 6, 1906; Rockhill to Gilbert Reid, July 16, 1906, Department of State Archives.
33. Reid to Rockhill, July 2, 1906, Department of State Archives.
34. Messrs., Seaman, Rudy, and Thomas to Reid, June 25, 1906, Department of State Archives.
35. Rockhill to Root, July 16, 1906, Enclosure No. 3, Memorandum left at Wai-wu Pu, July 13, 1906, by Rockhill, Department of State Archives.
36. Thomas Sammons, Consul-General in Newchwang, to Rockhill, July 12, 1906, Department of State Archives.
37. *Ibid.*
38. *Ibid.*
39. Rockhill to Root, July 31, 1906, Department of State Archives.
40. *Ibid.*
41. *Ibid.*
42. Rockhill to Hippisley, July 6, 1906, Rockhill Papers.
43. Sammons to Rockhill, July 12, 1906, Department of State Archives.
44. Adee to Rockhill, August 29, 1906, Department of State Archives.
45. Sammons to Rockhill, July 12, 1906, Department of State Archives.
46. *Ibid.*
47. *Ibid.*
48. Rockhill to Root, August 15, 1906, Department of State Archives.
49. *Ibid.*
50. *Ibid.*
51. *Ibid.*
52. Rockhill to Root, September 3, 1906, Department of State Archives.
53. *Ibid.*

54. Rockhill to Root, December 18, 1906, Department of State Archives.
55. *Ibid.*
56. *Ibid.*, October 11, 1906, Department of State Archives.
57. Roger S. Greene, Consul in Dairen, to the Assistant Secretary of State, January 29, 1908, Department of State Archives.

CHAPTER IX

THE FRUSTRATIONS OF INVOLVEMENT

S ECRETARIES of State Elihu Root and Philander C. Knox fully accepted the desirability of a China market open to all on an equal basis and the preservation of China's independence and territorial and administrative integrity. Their efforts in furthering these aims often won them reputations abroad for being provocative, aggressive and meddling in the affairs of others.

The testing ground was Manchuria. Although American diplomats showed restraint in judging the activities of both Russia and Japan in the two years following the signing of the Peace Treaty, uneasiness did not disappear. The Japanese lived and did business in areas far removed from the treaty ports without regard to treaty stipulations. They gained command of a large sector of the market for cotton goods by means of subsidized syndicates, subsidized shipping, government assistance in providing credit, and differential railway rates.

The Roosevelt Administration was fully aware of developments in Manchuria. Rockhill never assumed an attitude of hostility to Japan but he did present some disturbing facts. In May, 1907, he wrote to Secretary Root informing him that according to the annual report of the Imperial Maritime Customs Service, "Japanese products valued at £2,600,000 were imported into Manchuria, of which only £300,000 worth passed through Newchwang, where they were subject to import duty—the balance entering duty free." [1] Three months later Rockhill informed Elihu Root that the Japanese Minister

> admitted to me in a conversation that the retention, after the evacuation of Manchuria, by Japan of all land acquired by its military authorities at that place (Antung) was quite inconsistent with Japan's promise to China in the treaty of December, 1905;

that it prevented China and the United States from agreeing on the location of an international settlement at that port, and that something must be done to restore to China the property there taken. . . .[2]

Instead of rectifying this situation, wrote Rockhill, the Japanese were seizing more land.

In Mukden, young Willard Straight, who had developed a deep hostility toward the Japanese as Consul in Seoul before the Japanese take-over of Korea, reported with regularity on alleged Japanese violations of the Open Door. In May, 1907, he urged that Charles J. Arnell, Vice-Consul in Mukden, be sent to Antung to observe the Japanese.[3] A few weeks later, Straight wrote at length of the brusqueness of Japanese in seizing timber without paying for it and he expressed the view that they did so in the hope of an incident which they could exploit for gaining a sixty-year lease for lumbering in the region of the Yalu River. The Japanese, Straight also charged, sought control over the Penhsihu collieries.[4]

These fears were held in restraint until the early months of 1908 when Secretary of State Root, quite innocent of the provocative nature of the inquiries he set forth, became involved in a tangle of major proportions and of great historical significance. The issue concerned Harbin, the railway center in northern Manchuria. A more unlikely spot for the United States to become involved in a serious controversy would have been difficult to imagine for no Americans, except the American Consul, resided there and there were no American commercial interests in the town. Its population consisted of approximately sixty-two thousand Russians and thirty-three thousand Chinese.[5] Great Britain did not view Harbin as of sufficient importance to warrant stationing a Consul there. The importance of the city rested upon its location at the junction of the Chinese Eastern Railway and the railway running southward through Manchuria, the northern section belonging to Russia and the southern to Japan. Harbin, especially after the Russo-Japanese War, was famous for its disorderly elements, remnants of bonanza seekers, criminals, and brothels.

It was this disorder that led the more stable part of the population to demand the establishment of an effective municipal government. China had declared Harbin a treaty port in 1906 but in reality the only Harbin that was in existence was on land owned by the Chinese Eastern Railway. This ownership included lands some distance from the railway and in no way necessary to its operation. Harbin was a company town, and when the proposals for new municipal regulations were drafted, the hand of the company was clearly visible. It was the company that would indirectly exercise political powers and it would do so over Russians, Chinese, and any of the other nationalities or enterprises owned by those nationals. Although Harbin was nominally Chinese territory and in spite of the fact that under the treaties foreigners residing there were entitled to the right of extraterritoriality, a Russian company was to exercise both police and judicial powers, and the power to tax.

At first glance it would appear that the diplomatic contest was waged in behalf of the legal rights of Americans although no Americans were in residence. This was not the case. The diplomatic correspondence did not concern itself with the direct legal question involved but with the possible results, far from Harbin, if the United States, by remaining silent, acknowledged the rightness of what was taking place.

The question was brought to the attention of the Department of State by Fred Fisher, the Consul in Harbin, in a letter written in late December of 1907.[6] Willard Straight, Consul-General in Mukden, strongly endorsed Fisher's stand. He saw the importance of the question to lie in its influence on the Japanese who had not yet established governments in the towns along the South Manchuria Railway.[7] At the close of January, 1908, Henry Fletcher, Chargé d'Affaires in Peking, wrote that the Russian Minister had called his attention to Fisher's opposition to the municipal regulations. Fletcher reported: "He adverted to the fact that there were but 'one and a half' American citizens there and that our interests in Harbin did not seem to justify the active opposition of our consul." "He also stated," Fletcher recorded, "that if Americans 'put a spoke in the Russian wheel' there by giving the Chinese back bone, it certainly would not tend toward a friendly feeling and the time would come when it would be their turn, if Americans came then to trade, *et cetera.*"[8]

Russia's resentment was reaffirmed in a note from its Embassy in Washington to Secretary of State Root. The message charged that Fred Fisher sided with the Chinese in their protest against the proposed municipal regulation. This note obviously called for an answer, and it was at this point that the official American position was formulated. William Phillips, the very young and also very able Third Assistant Secretary, analyzed the problem and came forth with three conclusions. The proposal set forth at Harbin, he wrote, presented the question "whether we shall recognize the sovereignty of China or Russia in this disputed piece of territory." "If we recognize Russia's sovereignty," Phillips observed, "we must logically forfeit our extraterritorial rights at Harbin." China, he thought, "would have a good cause of complaint against the United States should we now accept the Russian point of view which, it cannot be denied, affects China's sovereignty in this region." Phillips observed that the United States was the only disinterested Power represented at Harbin. Both Japan and France desired enforcement of the railway regulations, and, in conclusion Phillips pointed out, "Japan is undoubtedly waiting for the moment to enforce a similar proposition in Southern Manchuria." [9]

Phillips saw great danger in acquiescence. Russia and Japan would establish "large foreign and commercial cities within Manchuria wholly independent of China. . . . The integrity of China would then be at an end," he warned.[10]

Root accepted Phillips' conclusions and embodied them in a reply to the Russian protest on April 9. He added to Phillips' case that Russia, in basing her claim on the provision in the Treaty with China of 1896 which acknowledged the right of the railroad to provide for administration of the land bordering the line, had extended the true intent of the provision. Clearly, said Root, this was not intended to bestow sovereign rights on the company. The provision intended no more than to give the railway the right to administer the land adjacent to the line and necessary for its operation.[11]

By April, 1908, the fire had reached the fat of Root's and Phillips' innocent logic on the enlarged significance of the Harbin municipal regulations. United States Ambassador in St. Petersburg, Montgomery Schuyler, on April 4 wired the Secretary asking for further information on the Harbin question, adding: "Prompt action desirable in view of the excitement here our alleged attempt of the Government of the United States to influence Russian policy in Manchuria. Three leading articles in the newspapers today." [12]

Root sought the support of other interested Governments. Copies of his note to Russia were forwarded to London, Berlin, and Tokyo.

Japan made it clear that she supported Russia. The Japanese Consul in Harbin, Fisher reported, was hard at work seeking the adoption of the proposed regulations, and on April 23, Japan's Ambassador in Washington presented Root with a memorandum in which Japan claimed, on the basis of treaties, that she had the right to exercise police authority in her railway zone in southern Manchuria.[13]

In the middle of April Root received word from Ambassador Thomas O'Brien in Tokyo giving Japanese reactions. He enclosed a clipping of an editorial expressing deep concern over the position the United States was taking on Harbin and giving voice to the fear that the United States would pursue a similar course over Mukden and other cities in the Japanese sphere. Also included was an editorial from another newspaper stating: "America's protest is not a warning against any violation of treaty stipulations. She seems to mean to take part in all questions and to interfere with other countries' activity, thereby to back up China's claims and advance her own influence." [14]

Similar warnings of strong opposition arrived from the American Embassy in St. Petersburg. Schuyler reported: "Much public excitement was caused here by the reports of the interference of the United States in a matter which the Russian government desired to be considered as purely of local importance." [15]

By the middle of May, Root was busily seeking the support of London and Berlin. Whitelaw Reid, Ambassador to Great Britain, discussed the question fully with Sir Edward Gray and found him sharing the American point of view on the legalities involved. Reid also, in accordance with instructions, questioned Gray as to whether he had any information about a secret agreement between Russia and Japan. Gray brushed this off with the speculation that their cooperation was due only "to the obvious community of interest between Russia and Japan looking to a possible assertion by those Governments of various corresponding pretentions in Northern and Southern Manchuria." [16]

The obvious cooperation of Russia and Japan and the dangerous prospect of facing this combination while still isolated diplomatically aroused a degree of anxiety among the staff in the State Department. In the midst of this, on June 9, arrived an extremely sharp note from Russia protesting Fisher's alleged support of the Chinese in Harbin and in a veiled fashion asking for his recall. Several of Root's assistants thought a reply should be delayed until German and British support had been assured.

The dispute had clearly moved into a major controversy, and Root now assumed full leadership. He prepared a memorandum for Alvey A. Adee as a guide to those charged with drafting a reply. He thought the situation called for a polite but firm answer and a promise that an inquiry would be made as to what action Fisher had taken and the precise nature of the policy he had advocated. However, the note should also state that it was believed that Fisher correctly represented the position of the Department.[17]

To these observations Root added a forthright estimate of the long-term course to be followed. The United States, he wrote, did "not purpose to surrender treaty rights in China or to concede that its sympathy can be excluded from those rights or subjected to any governmental power on the part of the Chinese railway company." [18]

However, at this point, much as John Hay had done when the war clouds gathered over Manchuria in the summer of 1903, Elihu Root struck a note of caution. His memorandum to Adee closed by putting the dispute into the perspective of the actual interests at stake:

> On the other hand we do not wish to be bumptious or disputatious or unfriendly in the assertion of our rights, or to become a protagonist in Manchuria, taking the responsibility of carrying on a vexatious controversy with Russia. A quiet, firm, maintenance of our position is our true policy and in that the interests to be preserved are the future interests of the open door and there is no present interest which would justify us in exhibiting undue excitement in this quiet and firm maintenance of our position.[19]

Root added that Great Britain and Germany concurred, "and that being so we need not fear that we are really going to lose anything."

Root had in his perceptive and lucid way caught in a few words the essential nature of his country's relationship to China.

There was no present interest that would justify "undue excitement." The interest was one that related to the future and this future interest justified the United States in retaining a voice in Far Eastern affairs so that when the interest became real it could be protected.

The Harbin question lingered on the agenda for another two years. The Department of State did not yield on the position that it had taken; neither did it aggressively pursue the matter. It also reconciled itself to accepting Japan's dominance of the railway towns in southern Manchuria, and when Russia questioned why it differentiated between what she did and what Japan did, the United States as quietly and unobstrusively as possible gave the evasive reply that in the case of Harbin a private company laid claim to sovereign powers while to the south it was the Government of Japan that exercised these powers.[20]

Root would not again permit adherence to the principles of the Open Door to entrap his Government in a dangerous showdown over the Manchurian issue. Throughout the Harbin dispute Root had continued to entertain the hope that Japan could be brought around to an acceptance of the American position. Now that the Harbin question had been put on the shelf, he entered into discussions with Ambassador Takahira in Washington with the aim of reaching a *modus vivendi*.

In November, 1908, Root and Ambassador Takahira completed their well-known agreement. At one time, historians saw in the agreement the granting of a free hand to Japan in Manchuria. A more recent interpretation more in harmony with the facts holds: "The exchange, rather, was just an air-clearing joint declaration of policy designed to smooth over the ill will which had been generated during the school segregation and immigration crisis of 1906 and war scare of 1907." [21]

In March, 1909, William Howard Taft became President and Philander Knox became Secretary of State. Taft had an interest in the Far East that grew out of his experience as Governor of the Philippines and a tour of China and Japan in 1905. His Secretary of State, a former Attorney General under Theodore Roosevelt, had no background in diplomacy nor had he manifested any previous interest in Asia. He received a memorandum from the Roosevelt Administration outlining the policies it had pursued.

The Administration, according to the document, had "given the strongest support to the securing to American interests of a one-fourth share in the very important railway loan in which Great Britain, France and Germany participate." The importance of this step, said the memorandum, "lies in the fact that it is a practical, material application of the principle and theory of the open door policy." The outgoing Administration, added the author, had likewise kept a jealous watch on imports into Manchuria in order to make sure that American exporters did not suffer discrimination by Foreign Governments. Finally, the Administration had stood firm in the controversy with Russia, opposing the bestowal of political rights on the Chinese Eastern Railway to Harbin.[22]

Before Knox had determined on a course of action, two of his assistants in the State Department, Willard Straight and Huntington Wilson, took the lead in demanding that a group of American bankers be admitted to participation in the financing of the Hukuang railway system in Central China. A consortium of European bankers, after difficult and prolonged negotiations, were about to sign a final agreement when Straight and Wilson upset their plans. This bold stroke proved to be the harbinger of Knox's New Dollar Diplomacy.

In June, 1909, Knox received a proposal from Henry Fletcher, Chargé d'Affaires in Peking. "There has been a feeling among Chinese officials," wrote Fletcher, "that American capital should be localized in Manchuria and that by placing it there they would be able the more readily to use our influence against Japan." Fletcher thought it would not be "to our best interests to enter this field alone." However, said Fletcher, if "an understanding be reached between the American, British, German, and French financial groups with regard to business in China, Manchuria will offer a promising field and from both the commercial and the political point of view it will be advantageous to all concerned to have concrete international financial interests in this section."[23]

Knox did not put his own conclusions in writing until Octo-

ber 8. The new Secretary of State made no mention of either
Japan or Manchuria at this time but the proposal he put forth
did have relevance to the problem there. He concluded that
wherever the Imperial credit of China was pledged for railway
construction, all of the Powers pledged to the Open Door "have
such a direct interest as to entitle them to participation in the
loans and equitable consideration for their nationals and mate-
rials." Likewise, he wrote, "in no case where a railroad is constructed upon Imperial credit or pledge of provincial revenues
should exclusive rights be granted to the nationals of any country
to do business of any kind within the territory served by railroad." [24] So far Knox merely sought to update the Open Door
Policy and make it relevant to the new situation. Not until
October 18 did he call for an inquiry as to the nature of "our
interest in Manchurian matters." [25]

Some members of the State Department had moved a long
way toward the position that measures should be taken to hold
off the Japanese from control of southern Manchuria and that
this could best be done by balancing off Japan's economic enterprises with investments, either American and British or by a
broader community of financial interests. The shift toward investment and opposition to Japan that took place in Washington
appears to have been more the product of those charged with
responsibility with foreign affairs within the Government than
of the bankers' interests. However, bankers now looking for
places to invest, missionaries, and journalists were not only willing partners but to some degree they had taken the initiative.

What pressures were there in the American community that
may explain, in part, the decision of Secretary of State Knox to
depart from Root's policy of restraint and to challenge both
Japan and Russia? Was this decision forced upon him by political
pressure? Or, did Knox embark on his diplomatic adventure as
unmindful of the domestic public pulse as he was of the degree
of determination both Russia and Japan had displayed during
the Harbin crisis?

William Phillips' letter to Rockhill in June, 1908, is evidence of an interest by bankers in China. Their interest preceded
Willard Straight's return to Washington and his efforts to encourage the bankers to invest. The group of banks organized

by the State Department to participate in the Hukuang loans were not the only ones showing an interest. Edward Harriman had led the way. The Hawley-Macy Syndicate employed F. V. Cloud, Straight's successor in Mukden, as its agent and actively sought investment opportunities.[26]

A few scattered journalists, friendly to China and hostile to Japan, encouraged friendship for China and portrayed in dramatic terms the power struggle taking place. The two foremost, Thomas F. Millard and Frederick McCormick, spent many years in China and to a considerable degree absorbed the Chinese point of view on the actions of the Japanese and the economic penetration of China by Europeans. Both understood the importance of contemporary alliances and the impact of these on China as well as their paralyzing effect on the attempts of the United States to influence the situation. Yet, the impact of Millard and McCormick before 1909 was certainly limited.[27] George Bronson Rea and the *Far Eastern Review* provided excellent factual accounts of the economic hold on China of the European Powers and Japan, but Rea did not crusade against Japan nor was he a promoter of a more active U.S. policy.

Of the various groups to which one looks in seeking to explain whence came the impetus for a stronger policy, the missionaries stand forth as the most energetic and vocal. Arthur H. Smith, the most popular writer on China among the missionaries, contributed largely to the fund of goodwill toward China and he also promoted a fear of what he called the "Japanization" of Asia.[28]

Smith's efforts were surpassed by those of Bishop William Bashford, former President of Ohio Wesleyan University, who went to China in 1905. Bashford soon became China's most effective spokesman in the American church community. An able writer and an eloquent speaker, he brought to the whole China question a fiery moral righteousness unhinged from any responsible assessment of the power factors. In 1908, Bashford marched straight to Washington and appealed to both Roosevelt and Taft. In his diary, Bashford recorded his conversation with Taft as follows: "I asked him as I had President Roosevelt, and Secretary Root, to use all his power short of going to war to preserve the integrity of Manchuria." The Bishop noted that

Roosevelt had said that "he was afraid to threaten war in case Japanese and Russians did not evacuate Manchuria lest they call his bluff." Continuing his report of his interviews, Bashford wrote, "I suggested both to him and to Mr. Taft that they get Germany, England and France to unite with United States in supporting Chinese claim and the integrity of her empire." According to the Bishop, "Taft went beyond President Roosevelt and thought he could get the other powers to join us in the matter and also thought it might be wise to give notice that we should support China by arms if necessary in maintaining her integrity."[29] Other missionaries lacked access to high places but they sided with China in an uncompromising spirit and looked to the United States to rectify what they held to be wrong.

This scarcely constituted a broad basis of support for the new viewpoint that had taken hold in the Department of State. Moreover, it was counterbalanced by the persistency of the old friendship for Japan. At the close of the Russo-Japanese War, Japan's popularity reached a peak. She had fought to defend her own interests but she had likewise fought for the Open Door in China. Her aims and those of the United States, contended many editors, were identical. Japan went to war, according to the *Journal of Commerce,* to defend freedom of trade and her statesmen were irrevocably committed to this principle. Russia, on the other hand, represented absolute despotism, an antiquated social order, and she had sought to take over Manchuria and from there to control Peking.[30] This black and white picture altered only slightly as wartime emotions receded.

Friends of Japan admired her surge toward a modern society and the energy the Japanese displayed. They saw no reason for being critical when this energy was directed towards Manchuria and they held it foolish to question her over taking full advantage of the rights she had acquired. Fear of Japan, said the *Journal of Commerce,* represented a "shallow kind of reasoning." "It will take the world some time to realize," said the editor, "how much it owes to Japan for demonstrating the hollowness and weakness of Russian autocracy and for turning back the shadow which it cast on the dial of time." "The real peril of Asia," he wrote, "was not a yellow but a white peril, and no nation has such profound cause for thankfulness that it exists no longer as the United States." To this he appended the non sequitur, "we are the greatest of the powers of the Pacific, and the rest of the world is beginning to recognize the fact that the North Pacific is already an American sea." [31]

The *Journal of Commerce* maintained its line of applauding Japan throughout 1906 and 1907 in spite of the reports of what the Japanese were doing in Manchuria and of the surge of hostility when the San Francisco School Board, in April, 1905, ordered that Japanese attend separate schools, an act that set off a two-year controversy over the question of Japanese immigration. It was true, the editor acknowledged, that the Japanese military had continued its hold on Manchuria to the advantage of Japanese merchants, but at a recent meeting of high officials, allegiance to the Open Door was reaffirmed. There was no reason to fear Japanese competition in the sale of cotton goods for Japan was not an important textile manufacturer. Even more important, Japan's heavy indebtedness and consequent dependence on foreign capital "will deepen the conviction that the only safe policy for Japan is to maintain, with absolute good faith, the principle of equality of commercial opportunity within the entire sphere of her influence." [32] The hostility between Americans and Japanese stemming from the demand of the Pacific Coast states that Japanese be barred from entry prompted a repetition of these arguments and the editor said that only "blatherkites and incendiaries" kept the war talk alive.[33]

The *Journal of Commerce* continued to adhere to this editorial position. In January, 1908, Japan was praised for energetically promoting her trade on the mainland by making loans available at low rates to the textile syndicate handling sales in China and by promoting low shipping rates. The editor did not usually approve of such practices but in this case it had been necessary by China's failure to establish a stable currency.[34] The Japanese Government's assistance in taking over the market in Manchuria elicited another detailed editorial account in August, 1909.[35] Again, there was no criticism of this policy. Other editorials in September and October of 1909 defended Japan.[36] When Japan objected to China building the Fakumen Railway on grounds of a secret article in the treaty negotiated by the two countries, in 1905, the editor held that Japan was justified in looking "beyond her own borders for the conditions of her national safety."[37] It was Japan, the editor wished to remind his readers, who saved the Open Door by defeating Russia and the question as to whether Japan threatened the Open Door now should be approached broadly. Again in April, 1910, the editor ridiculed the inevitability of war with Japan. The editor dismissed as pure nonsense the talk that Japan's efforts to capture markets affected control of the Pacific and menaced the peace of the world.[38]

The editors of the *Review of Reviews* and the *Outlook* gave no more support to the shift taking place in Washington than did the *Journal of Commerce.* "The Folly of War Talk," an editorial in the August, 1907, issue of the *Review of Reviews* adamantly declared, "that there does not now exist, nor has there ever existed, any cause of war whatsoever between Japan and the United States." To mention the possibility "is ridiculous, and to suggest it as likely would seem to indicate either a malevolent mind or a feeble understanding."[39] Again in March, 1908, the editor denounced talk of a conflict: "We have absolutely no grievance against Japan, and she has none whatever against us."[40] Shortly after both Russia and Japan rejected the Knox Neutralization Proposal in January, 1910, the *Review of Reviews* asserted: "It has been chiefly Russia's unwillingness to forego, or compromise in any way, the treaty privilege claimed under the agreements with China in 1896 and 1898 that has been responsible for the tangled condition of Manchurian economic and financial affairs during the past two years."[41]

Lyman Abbott, editor of the *Outlook,* eschewed an anti-Japanese line with equal consistency. He dismissed those who talked of war with Japan as a "small group of chauvinistic Americans." Only if they should get out of hand was there danger. Russia, not Japan, continued to serve as Abbott's pole star of evil among nations, and as late as October, 1910, he declared: "The most serious menace is Russia."[42]

Observing the relationship of the United States to the Manchurian question, a Briton, writing in the *North American Review,* said the American public had fallen into the habit of hostility to Japan and he thought there could "be little doubt that American diplomacy has acquired an anti-Japanese point, and that, as compared with five years ago, the misgivings entertained by the United States in regard to Japanese aims and policy, and the estrangement which has set in between the two peoples, must be reckoned as new factors in the Far Eastern situation." Yet, the same writer doubted that the public would support a war in defense of the proclaimed aims of their Government. A change was taking place but, he confessed, "so far as an outsider can judge, they have not yet thought the matter out." [43]

In the fall of 1909, the country was certainly not engaged in soul-searching on the China question. Only when an issue has been mulled over do sides emerge, and in October of that year there were no rival camps; only isolated individuals had identified their position. It was in this situation that Secretary of State Knox, so unlike his predecessors, Hay and Root, men of great aplomb, decided on a test case before knowing with any real assurance how it would be received abroad and with even less assurance that the American people would support him if the weather on the seas of diplomacy whipped up a storm.

The precise steps by which the neutralization proposal took form during the final weeks of October, 1909, are not known. This is a pity for it went beyond Knox's more cautious earlier analysis. By November 6, the proposal calling for an international loan to China enabling her to buy the foreign-owned railroads in Manchuria was ready and on its way. Attached to it was an alternate proposal for construction, with American and British capital, of a line from Chinchow to Aigun. The daring presumption that either Japan or Russia would dispose of the investments that meant so much to them or that they would not strenuously oppose the Chinchow-Aigun project is explicable only in relation to Russia. Knox's inquiries did suggest that there was a possibility, though remote, that Russia would sell the Chinese Eastern Railway because of the heavy financial losses of the company.[44] In relation to Japan no grounds existed for any such view. In fact, the reverse was true. Only a year before, Japan had vigorously opposed the building of the Fakumen line and in the course of that crisis, it had been revealed that China had agreed to a secret article in the treaty of December, 1905, not to construct any line parallel to the South Manchuria Railway.

Looking ahead, the neutralization proposal was rejected by

both Russia and Japan on January 21 in notes that indicated clearly that they had collaborated. In July, 1910, these two Powers signed an agreement which caused deep anxiety throughout China. In the course of this development both Great Britain and France supported their respective allies, Japan and Russia, so that it seemed that China faced a dangerous alignment opposed to Chinese aspirations to be masters of their own country.

The nations concerned rejected Knox's proposal with impunity, all parties recognizing that the United States was not prepared to go to the mat. The setback did not prevent the United States from launching a new project, a consortium of bankers to loan money to China. Again Japan and Russia objected to the original purpose, to provide funds for the Chinese to develop Manchuria. However, in a revised form the project was approved.[45]

Knox, like Hay and Root, retreated by the summer of 1910. Considerably less perceptive and less mindful of the realities than his predecessors, Knox had ventured further and persisted longer, but he too, at a late date, learned that present interests did not warrant excitement. Preserving a voice in Far Eastern affairs so that when American interests had passed from the realm of the potential to the real constituted American policy and the corollary to that policy stipulated that the United States should do no more than quietly reiterate the principles avoiding provocative measures.

NOTES

1. Rockhill to Root, May 17, 1907, Department of State Archives.
2. *Ibid.*, August 8, 1907.
3. Straight to Rockhill, May 2, 1907, Rockhill Papers, Harvard University Library.
4. *Ibid.*, June 14, 1907.
5. Fred Fisher to Assistant Secretary of State, November 25, 1906, Department of State Archives.
6. *Ibid.*, December 20, 1907.
7. Straight to Assistant Secretary of State, January 2, 1908, Department of State Archives.
8. Fletcher to Root, January 31, 1908, Department of State Archives.
9. Memorandum by William Phillips, Third Assistant Secretary, March 6, 1908, Department of State Archives.
10. *Ibid.*
11. Root to Russian Embassy, April 9, 1908, Department of State Archives.
12. Schuyler to Root, April 4, 1908, Department of State Archives.
13. Fisher to Assistant Secretary of State, April 15, 1908, and Takahira to Root, April 23, 1908, Department of State Archives.
14. O'Brien to Root, April 16, 1908, Department of State Archives.
15. Schuyler to Root, April 25, 1908, Department of State Archives.
16. In his acknowledgment of Reid's report, Root quoted from Reid's letter. Root to Reid, May 20, 1908, Department of State Archives.
17. Root to Adee, June 19, 1908, Department of State Archives.
18. *Ibid.*
19. *Ibid.*
20. Huntington Wilson to Fletcher, January 7, 1910.
21. Raymond A. Esthus, "The Changing Concept of the Open Door, 1899–1910," *The Mississippi Valley Historical Review*, XLVI (December, 1959), 450.
22. Memorandum to Philander Knox from the Roosevelt Administration, Correspondence of Philander C. Knox, Vol. VI, Knox Papers, Library of Congress.
23. Henry Fletcher to Knox, June 19, 1909, Knox Papers.
24. Knox to H. M. Hoyt, October 8, 1909, Knox Papers.
25. *Ibid.*, October 18, 1909.

26. Adee to William J. Calhoun, U.S. Minister to China, November 1, 1910, Department of State Archives.

27. Millard's book entitled *America and the Far Eastern Question* appeared in 1909. Many of his articles appeared earlier, but it was after the Knox Neutralization Proposal that he took his strongest stands. In an article entitled "America in China" published in *Forum* in July, 1910, Millard was critical not only of Japan and Russia but also of Great Britain. He thought the United States would have to reconsider permitting her naval supremacy. Regarding the control of railroads by Japan and Russia, Millard saw it as cutting across the interests of the United States and therefore the United States should be ready and willing to go to war if necessary.

28. Arthur H. Smith, "A Fool's Paradise," *The Outlook*, LXXXII (March, 1906), 706.

29. Unpublished diaries of William Bashford, Missionary Research Library, Union Theological Seminary.

30. Editor, "Foreign Politics and American Commerce," *The Journal of Commerce and Commercial Bulletin*, July 2, 1905, p. 2.

31. Editor, "Irresponsibility of Russia," *ibid.*, April 24, 1905, p. 4.

32. Editor, "Position and Policy of Japan," *ibid.*, May 28, 1906, p. 4.

33. Editor, "The Lines of Japanese Expansion," *ibid.*, March 25, 1907, p. 4.

34. Editor, "The Dominant Interest in the Far East," *ibid.*, August 23, 1909, p. 1.

35. "Japanese Competition Affects American Trade," *ibid.*, August 23, 1909, p. 1.

36. Editors, "New Treaty Between China and Japan," *ibid.*, September 6, 1909, p. 4 and "What Is At Stake in Manchuria," *ibid.*, October 18, 1909, p. 4.

37. Editor, "Japan and the Open Door in Manchuria," *ibid.*, October 25, 1909, p. 4.

38. Editor, "The Mastery of the Pacific," *ibid.*, April 4, 1910, p. 4.

39. Editor, "The Folly of War Talk," *The Review of Reviews*, XXXVI (August, 1907), 13.

40. Editor, "Japan and America," *ibid.*, XXXVII (March, 1908), 266–267.

41. Editor, "Secretary Knox's Manchurian Note," *ibid.*, XCL (February, 1910), 158.

42. Editor, "Will There Be War in the Far East," *The Outlook*, XCVI (October 1, 1910), 258–260.

43. Britannicus, "American Policy in the Far East," *The North American Review*, CXCII (September, 1910), 415–424.

44. *See* author's *Open Door Diplomat*, pp. 101, 102.

45. For an excellent detailed account of these negotiations, *see* Edward H. Zabriskie, *American–Russian Rivalry in the Far East: A Study in Diplomacy and Power Politics 1895–1914* (Philadelphia: University of Pennsylvania Press, 1946), pp. 152–160.

CHAPTER X
THE CHINESE REVOLUTION AND
THE AMERICAN RESPONSE

THE NEGOTIATIONS following the proposal of Secretary of State Knox took place as China headed toward revolution. A major aim of the revolution was to prevent foreigners from gaining economic control. Few of the many communications from the Legation failed to make note of the Chinese "rights recovery fever." In 1909 and 1910, the letters of Charles Tenney, Secretary of the Legation, described the new political movement in detail.[1] Tenney failed in only one respect, and understandably so. His reports gave no information on the more or less underground movement led by Sun Yat-sen. However, both he and the Minister, W. J. Calhoun, warned that foreign loans would meet strong opposition. The members of the old Manchu ruling caste, as one observer put it, welcomed loans from which they could replenish their private accounts, but these officials no longer represented China.

The Department of State acknowledged the reports of opposition but wrote them off as part of the traditional hostility to foreigners. Talk of revolution was difficult to assess. Popular movements had so long characterized China without culminating in revolution that there was a disinclination to take them seriously.[2] However, this time the Department miscalculated, although the reports from the many Consuls in various parts of the Empire and the tone of dispatches from the Legation should have warded off the error. In February, 1910, Chargé d'Affaires Fletcher cited the ground swell of Chinese opinion when he warned: ". . . they prefer that their country should lie fallow until such time as China can develop it herself, rather than that it should be exploited by foreigners."[3] Popular discontent fed by famine conditions led to local uprisings. In May, 1910, Vice-

Consul Albert Pontius in Suchien in Kiangsu reported the gathering of ten thousand people at a flour mill and burning it to the ground.[4] On May 25, 1910, the new Minister, W. J. Calhoun, wrote that the Throne was intent on yielding as little power as possible to the Constituent Assembly, and he thought a revolution inevitable.[5]

From Manchuria came other reports of deep resentment against the Japanese and pleas for American assistance. Wilbur J. Carr drafted a reply for the Secretary of State stating that it was most important for China to improve her administration, maintain order, encourage the development of the resources, and encouraging in every way the investment of foreign capital. As yet, the Department did not grasp how deeply opposed the Chinese were to investments by outsiders. However, Carr did recognize the limitations of the United States in seeking to assist the Chinese in their contest with Japan. The chief questions in Manchuria, wrote Carr, "are such that their solution depends primarily upon China itself." "This truth," wrote Carr, "cannot be too emphatically impressed upon the Chinese officials at the present time." In a plaintive note, reflecting the chastising effect of the rejection of the Knox proposal, Carr said, "The Chinese Government must know that this Government will not cease to give China its hearty moral support in the orderly development of the Manchurian provinces."[6]

Renewed warnings arrived in Washington in the summer of 1910 including a perceptive analysis by Calhoun stating that all would depend on the army and the army could not be relied upon to support the Central Government.[7] The Commander-in-Chief of the Asiatic Fleet, Rear Admiral John Hubbard, also thought that a revolution was inevitable. What would be the policy of the United States? he asked. Hubbard observed:

> While the really tangible American interests in China are relatively, and even actually, exceedingly small, it is supposed that there exists a certain looking ahead to future possibilities which must preclude any idea of our abandoning the fate of China entirely to other Foreign Powers. . . .[8]

In reply, Huntington Wilson said that the Department of State did not anticipate any serious uprising in China in the near future.[9]

Throughout the spring and summer of 1911, representatives of the United States repeated the same views many times. Whether the officials in Washington grasped the gravity of the situation is not clear. There was little they could do about it if it did come and there is no evidence to suggest that they cared whether the Manchus retained power, although they had no sympathy with the Chinese "rights recovery movement." In October, 1911, the Revolution burst forth and the Manchus collapsed almost at once. Early in 1912, the new Republic of China was proclaimed.

Within the next six months the question of recognition became a burning issue. If the dramatic days of the Boxer Revolt when so many American lives were in jeopardy be excepted, then no question relating to China had ever evoked so widespread an expression of friendship. The goodwill expressed suggested that a myth had grown up around China as a part of the world system of power. Sentiment, paternalism, even admiration for the Chinese among those Americans who knew them best were all elements in the public reaction. The sentiments that had furnished one of the several impulses in favor of a strong China policy and that played some immeasurable part in the stillborn scheme of Knox found in the new Republic a more attractive rallying point.

The support for recognition came from widely disparate sources and sections of the country. Five petitions came from local Chambers of Commerce, one of them from the national organization. Six originated in Rotary Clubs. Other commercial groups, including the American Asiatic Association, sent resolutions. Four well-known university and college Presidents, wrote to Washington, Nicholas Murray Butler of Columbia University, David Starr Jordan of Stanford University, Charles F. Thwing of Western Reserve University, and Henry Churchill King of Oberlin. A number of local Young Men's Christian Associations, women's clubs, and professors notified Washington of what should be done.[10]

Churches and missionary societies outnumbered all others and gave to the movement for recognition its fervor. In May, 1912, the General Conference of the Methodist Church met in Minneapolis. Two native Chinese, speaking through an interpreter, pleaded for the new Republic. The *Christian Advocate* described the scene that ensued:

It was a thrilling moment when these leaders from far-off China stood before their brethren and pleaded for the 'infant republic.' Patriotism and Christianity met and flowed on together, gathering power until the entire conference was upon its feet, cheering, shouting, and waving handkerchiefs. Hearts swelled and eyes grew dim as, in the midst of Dr. Wang's speech, someone started, 'My Country 'Tis of Thee.' How the great anthem bellowed and surged throughout the auditorium. The first republic and the last joined hearts and voices in a mighty burst of patriotic fervor as the audience rose to its feet and sang, as only Methodists can sing, 'Sweet Land of Liberty.'[11]

Bishop Bashford did more than arrange the staging of such scenes. He called on President Taft and urged him to recognize the new Government. Taft explained that he had entered into an agreement with the six Powers represented in the financial consortium that there be no intervention in China. Then, when Taft had proposed recognition, the other Powers said they would dissolve the agreement. Consequently, Taft concluded that he could serve China best by postponing recognition.[12]

The issue became confused in the public mind so that it was believed that it was the bankers who, seeking to drive a hard bargain with the new Government in Peking, caused the Governments to withhold recognition. This was not true. In fact, the consortium extended an emergency loan to the new regime to meet a pressing financial emergency. However, the Governments representing the bankers delayed granting recognition in the hope of having the new republican Government in Peking agree to provisions providing security for the loans. The debate continued throughout 1912 and the question of recognition had not been resolved when Woodrow Wilson took office in March, 1913. The Committee of Reference and Counsel of the Inter-denominational Conference of Foreign Missionary Boards sought to persuade President Wilson that he should recognize the new Government. At the same time the American banking group advised the Wilson Administration that it would continue only if requested to do so. On March 19, 1913, Wilson announced that he would not make such a request because the conditions laid down by the bankers "touch very nearly the administrative independence of China itself. . . ." On May 2, the United States recognized the Republic of China.

An era in the history of the relations between the Manchu-Chinese Government and the United States thereby came to a close. The heritage portended much for the future. A myth had grown up of the friendship of the United States for China and of the reservoir of goodwill in China for the United States. At no time had there been a clearly perceived national interest widely enough agreed upon to provide a basis for a strong China policy. Relations had been characterized by ambivalence. Generosity had been matched by insistence on retaining the old treaty system; the return of the Boxer indemnity and support for China in its efforts to free itself of the opium trade were accompanied by paternalism and a sense of superiority; and a hearty moral support was not matched by deeds. The United States, in spite of the absence of alliances, was inextricably tied into the whole system by which the outside world chose to maintain relations with China. It might have been more influential if it extricated itself completely from the system and accepted China as a full equal. It was powerless to do either. In the long run, it was China that had to restore order and achieve strength to remove the hold other nations had upon her. Because that struggle was so long and so bitterly fought, the Chinese emerged from it with lasting distrust.

NOTES

1. For Tenney's reports, *see Records of the Department of State Relating to Internal Affairs of China, 1910–1929.* The documents cited hereafter are from this collection.
2. Huntington Wilson to the Secretary of Navy, September 15, 1910.
3. Fletcher to Secretary of State Philander C. Knox, March 5, 1910.
4. Albert W. Pontius, Vice-Consul in Nanking, to Calhoun, May 4, 1910.
5. Calhoun to Secretary of State Philander C. Knox, May 25, 1910.
6. For Mr. Knox by Wilbur J. Carr to Fred Fisher, Consul-General in Mukden, July 18, 1910.
7. Calhoun to Secretary of State Philander C. Knox, July 5, 1910.
8. Rear Admiral John Hubbard, U.S.N., to the Secretary of Navy, July 26, 1910.
9. Huntington Wilson to the Secretary of Navy, September 15, 1910.
10. All of the letters are to be found in the *Records of the Department of State Relating to Internal Affairs of China, 1910–1929.*
11. Bashford to Secretary of State Philander C. Knox, includes clipping, May 15, 1912.
12. Bashford to Woodrow Wilson, November 28, 1912.

POSTSCRIPT 1968

SINCE John Hay's Open Door Notes, China has fascinated everyone interested in foreign affairs. Yet, no foreign policy question has so defied assessment of vital interests. Hay's Notes became the basis of a myth whereby it was generally believed that it was the policy of the United States to protect China against the Imperialistic Powers of Europe and a designing and ambitious Japan. Indeed, so it was said, Hay saved China from partition. The myth flourished and served as the lens through which Americans viewed their relations with China from the beginning of the century until the Communist take-over.

This myth stood in the way of our understanding the China policy of the Department of State—to say nothing of an understanding of China itself. China was weak and of little importance to the United States either as a market for surplus goods or in terms of security considerations. Our China policy reflected these basic facts, not the proclaimed friendship of the missionaries or the generous goodwill China enjoyed among large groups of Americans. The inversion of the myth, since 1949, into hostility toward China on the one hand and denunciation of our policy on the other, has now entrapped us.

China is a major divisive element in American political life. Yet, at a time when relations with China require some of our most important foreign policy decisions, there is little understanding of the problems that harass the Chinese and even less of U.S. policy in East Asia. It would be silly to claim that all could be made clear if men of goodwill would sit down and seek to understand. There are key questions to which there are no answers, and we must beware of treating the problem as though the right policy is either a full measure of militant patriotism or one of simple moral considerations.

Aside from seeking to analyze where China is heading, we face questions of how important American interests are in East Asia. Are we, without full awareness, slipping into a pattern of action leading to visions of a Pax Americana? Are we fighting to stop the spread of Communism as though we still faced a monolithic Communist bloc? Are we still opposed to admitting China to the United Nations or are there other issues in back of that question making a positive stance difficult? Would a hasty withdrawal from Vietnam result in China taking over the border states? These and many other questions impinge upon us and are not questions lending themselves to precise answers.

The problem immediately before us is to understand what has happened in China. The first ten years of Communist rule saw gains of all kinds—great achievements in the production of grain and steel, the building of factories and hydroelectric power plants. Production far surpassed anything that had been achieved under previous governments. For the first time famines were almost eliminated, thanks to better distribution. Great strides were made in public health.

Then, in 1958, came a new program—the Great Leap Forward. China faced a crisis in terms of the aims she had set for rapid industrialization. To achieve this, she launched a program of small industries throughout the countryside and drafted farm laborers from the communes to work in them. The results were more than disappointing—they were catastrophic. The goods produced were so inferior they were often unusable. At the same time, by taking labor out of agriculture, food production fell. The situation was made worse by a series of crop failures and the withdrawal of Russian aid. Industrial production dropped sharply as China could no longer export sufficient agricultural produce to buy industrial components.

There has been a period of recovery since 1962. At least there have not been serious food shortages. However, rapid economic development has not taken place. If we look at the statistics for agricultural output, we find that from 1953 to 1957 total grain production averaged one hundred and seventy-two million metric tons and it amounted to no more than one hundred and eighty-two million in 1964, an excellent harvest year. In the case of wheat, there was an actual decline in 1965 as compared to the middle fifties. Industry, too, was slow to recover, particularly heavy industry. Basically, China remains a poor nation struggling with every ounce of its energy to dispel poverty. Some idea of that poverty is suggested by the estimate that the average per capita income is seventy-five dollars per annum.

The Cultural Revolution, beginning in August, 1966, followed these setbacks. The Red Guards and the crusade against revisionism moved to the fore. Mao's new moves were designed to counteract hostile forces. He had lost control of the Central Committee of the Communist Party and faced the threat of a take-over by the Chairman, Liu Shao-ch'i. Mao was also disturbed by the rise of a new class of elite who, because of their education and skills, had moved into important positions in the bureaucracy. Among these were the teachers who were criticized for displaying aristocratic tendencies. China faced a major crisis among its youth, many of whom discovered that they did not feel at ease in schools where the stress was on academic achievement and where they found it difficult to compete with the sons and daughters of more favored families. Mao sympathized with these frustrated students and believed the Revolution must be extended so that the most humble parts of the population could participate in the building of the new China.

Other issues contributed to the clash between Mao and the Communist Party. The leadership was divided by the controversy with the Soviet Union and the resulting debate over the feasibility of pushing world revolution and wars of national liberation. Some leaders maintained that continued Soviet economic assistance was so important that it necessitated acceptance of the Soviet policy of peaceful coexistence. This foreign policy issue was closely related to the key domestic issue of whether it was more important to improve the standard of living or to extend the Revolution. Mao was committed to the latter and opposed the former as revisionism.

These circumstances led Mao to launch the Cultural Revolution in the summer of 1966. The Red Guards provided an ideal instrument. By enlisting students, he could provide them with the exhilarating experience of carrying out a revolution and endow them with revolutionary fervor. At the same time, the Red

Guards proved an effective weapon against the Party. Once the thousands—and at one point, more than a million—of students descended on Peking in search of bourgeois elements, the Party was helpless and Mao was soon able to depose the leaders including the Chairman, Liu Shao-ch'i. The Red Guards likewise sought out members of the new elite who had carved out comfortable and privileged positions for themselves in China's new society. Intellectuals, and especially teachers, were hunted out and assigned demeaning tasks such as latrine duty. In some cities the labor unions affiliated with the Party struck in retaliation. In Canton, for a time, families in various districts of the city set up their own guards to keep the Red Guards from coming in.

The battle was not over Communism. There was no question either of taking action against dissatisfied elements who might desire to overthrow the State and the Party. The State could readily suppress any anti-Communist opposition. Most workers in China are covered by a remarkably complete dossier that gives a report of their work and records any remarks that they may have made that had political overtones. This machinery is so all-embracing an instrument of social and political control that there is no fear of a movement against the State.

The Red Guards got completely out of control. The Mao Government found it necessary to turn to the army to restore order, and by the autumn of 1967 the army was the main arm of government. In turn, the effort to control the Cultural Revolution caused deep disillusionment among its supporters, especially the students. Young Maoists charged that their cause was being sold out and stories circulated in Peking that it might be necessary for Mao to flee to the mountains to carry on guerrilla warfare. Some followers talked of having to seize weapons from the army. So serious was this feeling, and so widespread, that late in 1967, Premier Chou En-lai found it necessary to make a special appeal to the disillusioned, assuring them that they would not be betrayed. There was no real prospect of any such event, but the necessary efforts to moderate the Cultural Revolution looked this way to the disappointed Red Guards.

Unrest and strife among factions of Mao supporters became so serious during the closing months of 1967 that Mao found it necessary to denounce these disagreements and urge the factions to find a common ground. Chou En-lai, in an effort to restore unity, dictated agreements to the disputing factions. These did not always satisfy the extremist groups, who protested that they should be permitted to maintain their own identity.

The outcome of these developments was unpredictable. The disturbances, the fragmentary reports on economic conditions indicated, had led to a decline in agricultural and especially industrial production. The tensions, though serious, might prove to be a passing phase in the development of the new society.

In the realm of foreign affairs a basic and persistent element in Chinese thinking about the outside world has been a deep distrust of all of the great powers. This hostility had deep roots and was at least reminiscent of the traditional, cultural introversion that prevailed under the Manchu Dynasty. It was also a legacy from the one hundred years of humiliation when China was weak and vulnerable to dictation from Japan and the great nations of Europe. Finally it was a product of revolutionary Communist ideology which divided the world into halves, the Socialist half being good and the Capitalist inherently imperialistic. These feelings were strengthened by the U.S. policy of containment. The hostility, while directed chiefly at the United States, extended to all foreigners.

The Chinese Communist world view was also embodied in the revolutionary theory that evolved out of the Communist strategy used in defeating the Kuomintang. Lin Piao, Minister for Defense and Mao's heir apparent, in a speech delivered in September, 1965, declared that the Communists had won the war by winning the support of the peasants. After gaining control of the countryside, they had isolated the cities and before long, the cities fell into their hands. Lin Piao outlined a parallel strategy for the world revolution. The underdeveloped countries would find in China the model they could follow in achieving economic growth and China would help them although they must win their own wars of national liberation. Then, when these underdeveloped countries had freed themselves from the dominance of the imperialist powers and no longer permitted the strong powers to exploit them, the imperialist nations, as had happened to the cities of China, would fall.

This was the Communist Chinese world view and their activities in Latin America and Africa represented its implementation. For a time, the Chinese did win friends but the violence of their views frightened many of the newly established governments. Chinese activity in the underdeveloped parts of the world appeared relatively unsuccessful by late 1967.

However satisfying as rhetoric, China's stated ambitions to lead the underdeveloped world provided a severe test of her economic capabilities. The assistance she provided was limited. In the long run, China was more likely to concern herself with the "bread and butter" problems of foreign policy security, friendly neighbors, prestige, markets, imports of what she needs for developing industry, and possibly capital. Like the Soviet Union in the years after the Revolution of 1917, China disdained traditional diplomacy and the institutions that provided some degree of order and security, but eventually China might find it necessary, as did the Soviet Union, to devote her major effort to achieving realistic and down-to-earth aims.

China's aims in Asia provoked uneasy speculation. In terms of history, of her culture, and of her population, China could be expected to seek dominance in Asia. That she believed that this was her rightful place seemed beyond question, but the kind of relationship she envisioned was subject to debate. Some argued that she would move into the countries of the area and govern them directly. Others, consulting China's record, believed that her aim was to promote friendly Communist states. China's attempt, in 1965, to overthrow the Government of Indonesia and to establish a regime that would be a close ally reflected her new ambitions. The fact that there were committees in Peking whose declared purpose was to sponsor revolutions in Thailand and Malaya, pointed in the same direction. And, in Thailand and Burma, and also in Laos and Cambodia, there were insurrectionary forces that had been trained in China.

On the other hand there was also evidence that China aimed at less than the overrunning of these states. She had pursued a cautious, rather than an adventurous, policy toward them. She might well be content to have her neighbors as client states, for the Chinese were fully aware of the costs and the headaches the Soviet Union experienced with the satellite countries of Eastern Europe. However, few doubted that at the minimum she would endeavor to force the countries of East and Southeast Asia to support Chinese foreign policy, especially her posture of hostility to the United States. And China, as a nuclear power, was in a strong position to threaten any neighboring government that went contrary to her wishes.

The U.S. response to the new China was outlined by Undersecretary of State Nicholas Katzenbach in an address delivered on November 27, 1967. He repeated time and again the words "engagement," "containment," and "peace." These embodied the basic approach of his Government to the whole question of Asia. Engagement applied to the determination of the Administration of Lyndon Johnson not to retreat to isolationism. Containment represented the many treaties of defense the United States had entered into with the aim of providing a shield behind which these countries could develop stronger economies and stable governments. Finally, the Undersecretary used the term "peace." He had in mind the importance of nonmilitary aspects of long-term policy when he said:

> It would not be visionary, I think, to hope for some change some-day in the view of Communist China's leaders, too. In the meantime, the United States must be prepared to work toward ways of living with Peking, however difficult that job seems today. We have already suggested—and must keep suggesting—those steps which would increase contacts and communications.

We must, he said, pursue "the difficult task of building bridges of peaceful cooperation with those who would be our enemies."

In his State of the Union message President Johnson again affirmed that the shield must be maintained while the United States at the same time sought to impress the Peking Government that there were alternatives if Peking chose to modify her policy of a closed door to all exchanges. The President pointed to the removal of the barrier against the journalists of both countries having access to the other. He emphasized the willingness of the United States to restore trade relations.

There was little reason to hope that China would respond to these gestures. Only an immediate and complete withdrawal of U.S. support of Taiwan could be counted upon to change China's hostile posture. The United States, committed to Taiwan by the Mutual Defense Pact of 1954, would probably have accepted a two-China arrangement but no more. Both Chinese Governments rejected this proposed solution. The Government on Taiwan threatened to pull out of the United Nations if the Peoples' Republic of China were admitted.

The Administration of Lyndon Johnson confronted considerations that seemed not to enter into the thinking of the Doves and the Hawks, the two extremes in the public debate over the U.S. involvement in Vietnam. A withdrawal from Vietnam would in all likelihood result in direct confrontation with China elsewhere in Asia and should this take place it would be even more difficult to hold in restraint the potentially dangerous nationalistic sentiments that would have been aroused. Consequently a withdrawal from Vietnam, short of a settlement that assured some stability in the area, raised the prospect of a war of larger proportions.

Another alternative was large-scale disengagement from Asia. This would mean a repudiation of the many treaties with Asian countries. To do so would be to remove the very bases of the order that did exist and, consequently, open the way to the creation of a new order. In the process each of the Asian nations would find it necessary to work out new security arrangements, a process not unlikely to produce strife. The United States would find it difficult not to become involved in what would probably be a major war.

The risks of continued involvement in Vietnam until peace could be established was probably the least dangerous of these alternatives but it involved the risk of the fighting getting out of control and therefore collision with China.

INDEX